Insects in the Classroom

Insect activities for years 0-6

By Robinne Weiss

Insects in the Classroom

by Robinne Weiss

Copyright © 2017 by Robinne Weiss
Photographs by Robinne Weiss except where noted in the text

License notes:
This book is licensed for your personal use, or the use of your school, if it was purchased for the school resource library. You are welcome to make as many copies of the student worksheets as you need for your class. I understand that you may also want to share with colleagues. You are welcome to share one of the activities in this book, but please do not share more than this without purchasing another copy of the book for your colleague.

If you are reading this book and did not purchase it, or it was not purchased for your school, then please follow one of the author links below and purchase your own copy. The activities in this book are ones I developed over 25 years of teaching, and they represent many hours of work--thank you for respecting that work.

Discover other titles by Robinne Weiss by visiting my author pages:

Wordpress: https://robinneweiss.wordpress.com/stories-and-books/
Amazon.com: https://www.amazon.com/Robinne-Weiss/e/B01E65CCP0/ref=sr_ntt_srch_
  lnk_1?qid=1478034631&sr=8-1

Front cover photos (clockwise from top right): chorus cicada (*Amphipsalta zealandica*), yellow admiral butterfly pupa (*Vanessa itea*), New Zealand praying mantis (*Orthodera novaezealandiae*), katydid (*Caedicia simplex*)

Back cover photos (clockwise from top right): drone fly (*Eristalis tenax*), yellow admiral butterfly (*Vanessa itea*), burnt pine longhorn beetle (*Arhopalus tristis*), New Zealand praying mantis (*Orthodera novaezealandiae*)

Contents

Background Information 1
Bug Basics 2
- What is an Insect? 2
- External Anatomy 3
- Internal Anatomy 3
- Life Cycle and Development 4

Other Arthropods 6
- Spiders 6
- Harvestmen 6
- Slaters 6
- Pseudoscorpions 6
- Millipedes 6
- Centipedes 6
- Ticks and Mites 6
- Hoppers 6

Insect Classification 7
Insects in the Classroom--Why insects? 9
- Cost and Availability 9
- Time 9
- Importance to Humans 9
- Fascination 10
- Flexibility 10

Inviting Insects Onto the School Grounds 11
- Food 11
- Water 11
- Shelter 11
- Other Attractants 11

Caring for Insects in the Classroom 12
- Mealworm 12
- Slater 12
- Praying mantis 12
- Monarch butterfly 12

Activities/Lessons 13
- What is an Insect? 14
- Insect/Spider Puzzles 16
- Camouflage Game 21
- Chemical Warfare 23
- Habitat Mural 24
- Invertebrate Survey 25
- Insect Classification 26
- Honey Bee Dance 28
- My Favourite Food Is... 29
- Honey Bees In Trouble 35
- Measuring Diversity 38
- Cricket Olympics 42

Colouring Sheets 44
Worksheets / Puzzles...54
Identifying Insects 59
Resources 66
Glossary...68

Background Information

Bug Basics

What is an Insect?

Simply put, an insect is an arthropod which, as an adult, has six legs, three main body regions (head, thorax, and abdomen), and two antennae. Many adult insects also have two or four wings. Insects are the only arthropods with wings.

However, when it comes to arthropods, nothing is quite that simple. Some insects are legless, including many insect **larvae**; some larvae have extra leg-like appendages; and the distinctions between the three body regions are often difficult to see. And if that wasn't enough confusion, some six-legged creatures with three main body regions and two antennae are not insects.

Insects belong to the class Hexapoda (meaning six-legged). Within this class, there are currently 31 orders. Three of those orders are considered non-insect Hexapods, and the remaining 28 are the insects.

There is ongoing controversy over the insect orders. Which insects should be included in which orders? Which groupings should be given the status of order versus sub-order? Most of the controversy arises because we don't always understand the genetic relationships among insects, so whenever scientists learn something new about the evolution and relatedness of insects, it changes our classification of them.

To give you something to work with, below is a list of the Hexapod orders, as presented in *The Insects, 4th Ed* by Gulan and Cranston, 2010 (see Resources section for details).

Non-Insect Hexapods
Protura—proturans
Diplura—diplurans
Collembola—springtails, snowfleas

Insects
Archaeognatha—bristletails
Zygentoma—silverfish, firebrats
Ephemeroptera—mayflies
Odonata—dragonflies, damselflies
Grylloblattodea—rock crawlers
Phasmatodea—walkingsticks, timemas
Orthoptera—grasshoppers, crickets, wētā
Mantodea—mantids
Blattodea—cockroaches, termites
Mantophasmatodea—gladiators (this order was discovered in 2002)
Dermaptera—earwigs
Embioptera—webspinners
Plecoptera—stoneflies
Zoraptera—angel insects
Psocodea—lice
Hemiptera—true bugs, cicadas, hoppers, psyllids, aphids, whiteflies, scales
Thysanoptera—thrips
Neuroptera—lacewings, antlions
Megaloptera—alderflies, dobsonflies
Raphidioptera—snakeflies
Coleoptera—beetles
Strepsiptera—twisted-wing parasites
Mecoptera—scorpionflies
Siphonaptera—fleas
Diptera—flies
Trichoptera—caddisflies
Lepidoptera—butterflies, moths
Hymenoptera—wasps, bees, ants, sawflies

Within the 28 orders of insects, there are about a million identified species, and many more that haven't yet been described by scientists. There may be as many as 7.8 million species of insect on Earth.

As you can see, we have a lot to learn!

External Anatomy

With over a million species of insects in the world, no description of their features can encompass the full range of variation among them. There are exceptions to every rule. In general, the following is true about adult insect anatomy.

Exoskeleton

Like all arthropods, insects have an **exoskeleton**—a skeleton on the outside of the body. The exoskeleton not only provides support and a place for muscles to attach, but also protects the insect from predators, pathogens, and the environment. Exoskeletons can be incredibly tough; the exoskeleton of an insect's jaws (**mandibles**) can reach a hardness of 3 on Moh's scale of mineral hardness—the same as copper.

Head

The head is the sensory centre of an insect. On the head are the following:

Compound eyes—Compound eyes are composed of many individual **ommatidia**, each of which acts as an individual eye. Compound eyes cannot produce sharp, detailed images like our eyes do, but they are particularly good at detecting motion—an important trait for fast-flying insects, or for avoiding predators and fly swatters.

Ocelli—Many insects have three small eyes in addition to compound eyes. These eyes sit on the top of the head and play a role in regulating the insect's daily rhythms.

Antennae—Antennae are sensory appendages. They bristle with sensory neurons and hairs that can detect smells, touch, sounds, and tastes.

Mouthparts—Insect mouthparts vary wildly, from chewing mandibles in beetles, to scissor-like slicing mouthparts in horseflies, to straw-like mouthparts in moths and butterflies. Each type of mouthpart has evolved to exploit a particular food source.

Palps—Most insects have four palps arranged around their mouths. Palps feel and taste food before the insect eats it.

Thorax

The thorax is the locomotory centre of an insect. Legs and wings are attached to the thorax. Only adult insects have wings.

Abdomen

The abdomen houses the insect's reproductive system and much of its digestive system. Usually, there are no appendages on the abdomen except at the very tip. Female insects may have an **ovipositor** (an egg-laying tube) at the tip of their abdomens. In some insects (ants, bees and wasps) the ovipositor is modified into a sting. Two **cerci** might also be found on the tip of the abdomen. These are sensory organs, a bit like "rear view" antennae. Male insects may also have external genitalia visible on the tip of the abdomen.

Internal Anatomy

Circulatory System

Insect circulatory systems are open, meaning the **hemolymph** (blood) doesn't flow through blood vessels, but circulates loosely around the insect's body cavity. A muscular tube, the dorsal aorta, acts as a heart, circulating the hemolymph around the body. Like our blood, hemolymph carries nutrients, hormones, wastes, and immune defences. Unlike our blood, however, insect hemolymph does not carry oxygen (except in a few species). Hemolymph is also occasionally used as a chemical defence against predators. Ladybugs, for example, have hemolymph that smells and tastes bad. When threatened, they bleed from their leg joints, giving a predator a nasty mouthful.

Respiratory System

Insects do not have lungs. Holes in their abdomens (**spiracles**) lead to tubes called **trachea** that carry oxygen to all the cells in their bodies. Interestingly, trachea are lined with exoskeleton, so when the insect moults the trachea shed a layer, too. You can often see the larger trachea in the shed exoskeletons of cicadas and other large insects—they look like white strings attached to the inside of the abdomen.

Life Cycle and Development

An insect's life span can range from a matter of days to seventeen years. Most insects in temperate regions, however, have a life span of a year. Some notable exceptions are some of our wētā, which may live up to eight or nine years; our native cicadas, which spend up to three years as nymphs underground; and on the other end of the spectrum, many of our aphid pests, which have a generation time of about five days.

Insects go through **metamorphosis**—a dramatic change in body shape—during their life cycle. There are two types of metamorphosis—complete and incomplete.

Complete Metamorphosis

In **complete metamorphosis**, an insect's body changes *completely* from egg to adult. There are four stages in complete metamorphosis:

Egg—like chicken eggs, insect eggs contain the embryo of the new insect.

Larva—the young stage. This stage is focused on growth. It goes through several **instars**, or stages of growth between moulting. Most insects spend the majority of their lives as a larva.

Pupa—this is often described as the "resting stage", because a pupa has only limited or no mobility. It looks like nothing is happening, but inside the pupa, the insect's body is undergoing massive changes.

Adult—the reproductive stage of the insect. Adult insects often have wings (it is the only life stage with wings). The focus of this stage is on reproduction. In many insects, the adult stage is relatively short. In insects that go through complete metamorphosis, the larva and the adult often eat very different foods. Some insects do not eat as adults.

Examples of insects that go through complete metamorphosis are bees, wasps, ants, butterflies, moths, beetles, and flies.

Incomplete Metamorphosis

Incomplete metamorphosis is a simpler change than complete metamorphosis. There are only three stages.

Egg—like chicken eggs, insect eggs contain the embryo of the new insect.

Nymph—the young stage. The nymph hatches from the egg looking much like a miniature adult without wings. The nymphal stage is focused on growth and goes through several instars. Each instar looks more and more like the adult insect. Wing buds can be seen on nymphs, though the wings don't fully develop until the adult stage.

Adult—the reproductive stage of the insect. Adult insects often have wings (it is the only life stage with wings). The focus of this stage is on reproduction. In insects that go through incomplete metamorphosis, nymphs and adults usually eat the same foods.

Examples of insects that go through incomplete metamorphosis are grasshoppers, crickets, wētā, cicadas, aphids, stick insects, and praying mantids.

Growth and Moulting

An insect's exoskeleton does not grow once it has formed and hardened. For an insect to grow, it needs to shed its exoskeleton and grow a larger one (a bit like children who need new clothes as they grow out of their old ones). We call this process **moulting**.

When an insect moults, it finds a safe spot where it is protected from weather and predators. Its old exoskeleton splits down the back, and the insect crawls out of it.

The new exoskeleton has formed underneath the old, but when the insect first emerges from the old exoskeleton, the new one is pale, soft, and flexible. The insect expands the new exoskeleton while it is soft, often by gulping air or water. As the exoskeleton hardens, it darkens. Until the exoskeleton is hard, the insect has very limited movement (imagine if all your bones were soft instead of rigid), and is vulnerable to predators.

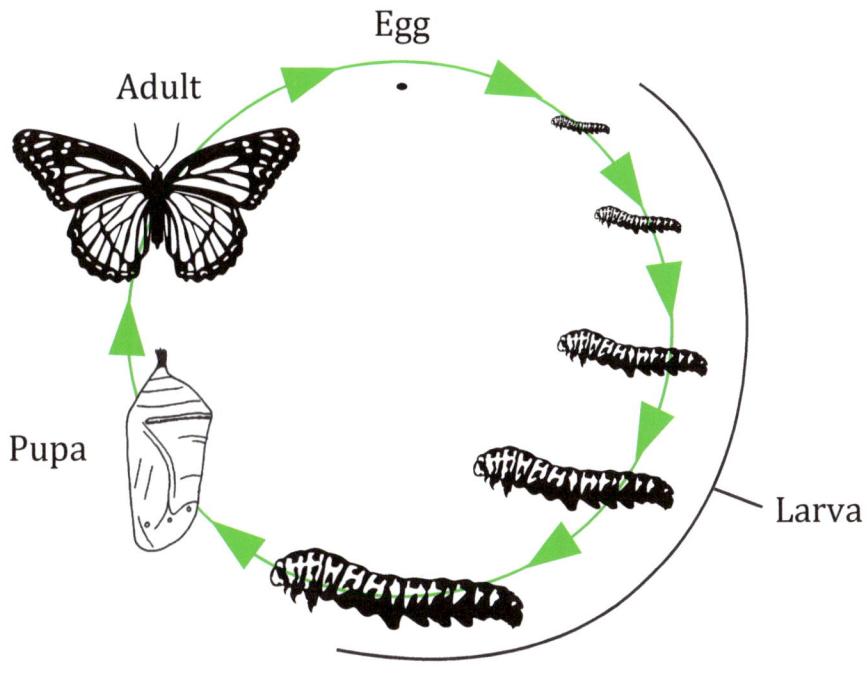

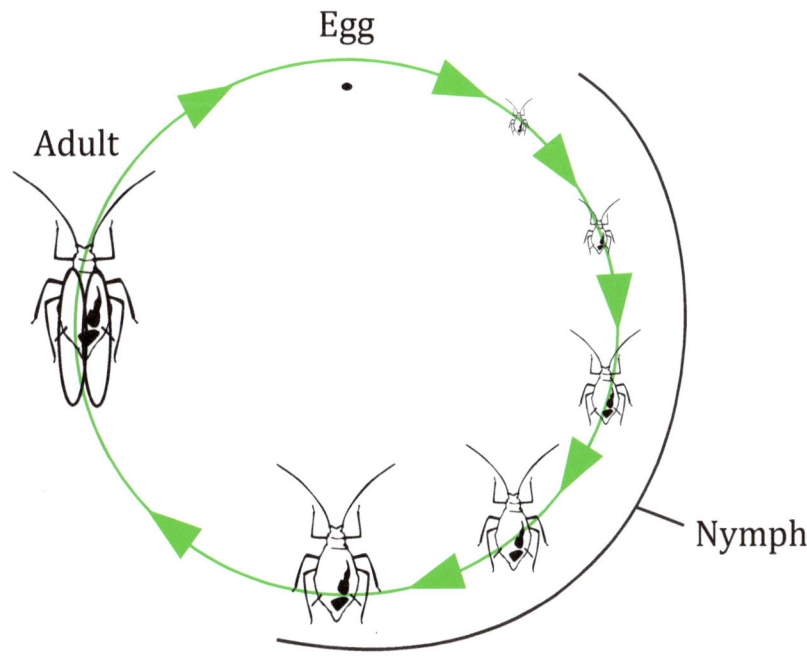

Insects In the Classroom 5

Other Arthropods

Many of the creatures you find in your backyard aren't insects, but are other **arthropods**. Below are a few of the more common ones. Photos and identification keys for these animals can be found in the Identifying Insects section on page 59.

Spiders

Spiders have eight legs, two main body regions (a **cephalothorax** and an abdomen), six or eight simple eyes, and no antennae. Spiders produce silk from **spinnerets** located on their abdomens. They use silk for prey capture, shelter, protecting their eggs, support and safety when climbing, and even for locomotion (a behaviour called **ballooning**). Almost all spiders are predators that subdue their prey with venom. There is only one herbivorous spider known.

Harvestmen

Harvestmen are often confused with spiders, as they have eight legs and no antennae. They only have one major body region, however, not two like spiders. Harvestmen eat dead or very small insects. They have no venom and do not spin silk.

Slaters

Slaters are also known as isopods, woodlice, pill bugs, sow bugs, roly polies, potato bugs, and a host of other names. Slaters are crustaceans, related to crabs and crayfish. They have 12 or 14 legs on segmented bodies. They have two pairs of antennae, but only one pair is easily seen. Like all crustaceans, slaters breathe through gills. To survive on land, they carry water with them, surrounding their gills.

Pseudoscorpions

These tiny arthropods are common in leaf litter, but are seldom seen. They resemble a miniature scorpion without a tail. Their two large pincers are used for grabbing the dead leaves and other detritus they eat.

Millipedes

Millipedes have a long, rope-like, segmented body. They have 25 to 100 pairs of legs, which sit largely underneath the body. They are generally slow-moving, and often curl up when threatened. Millipedes are scavengers, eating mostly dead plant material.

Centipedes

Centipedes have a long body like millipedes, but the body is flattened. Twenty-five to 100 pairs of legs arise from the sides of the body. Centipedes are fast moving and usually run when disturbed. They are predators on other invertebrates, and their first pair of legs is modified into a pair of poison fangs. Larger centipedes can give a sharp bite if handled roughly.

Ticks and Mites

Ticks and mites have two main body regions, but they often appear as one. They have eight short legs (six when newly hatched), and no antennae. Most are very small. They are a highly diverse group of arthropods including parasites, predators, and herbivores.

Hoppers

Hoppers are crustaceans, and look a lot like shrimp (though they live on land). They rarely sit still for identification, but rather are known by their behaviour—springing frantically away when disturbed. Sand hoppers are common on the beach, and land hoppers can often be found in moist areas under logs.

Insect Classification

Many people lump all creepy-crawlies into one category—bugs. That informal category can include animals as diverse as worms, spiders, insects, centipedes, and slaters. Unfortunately, the category is meaningless if we're trying to make sense of what "bugs" are, and how they're related. For example, earthworms are in the phylum Annelida, insects are in the phylum Arthropoda, and humans are in the phylum Chordata, all within the kingdom Animalia. By this measure, we are as likely as insects and worms to be "bugs."

The figure on the following page includes most of the familiar creepy-crawlies, giving you an idea of their **taxonomy** and diversity.

Some of the common creatures your students will ask about and be able to distinguish are included in the Identifying Insects section on page 59.

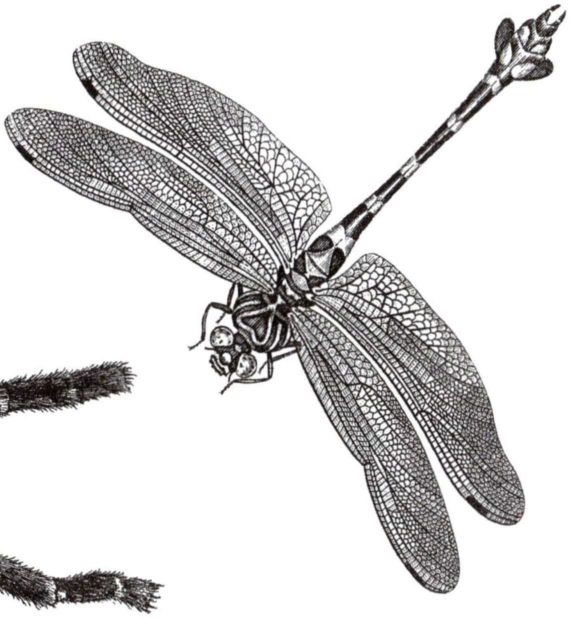

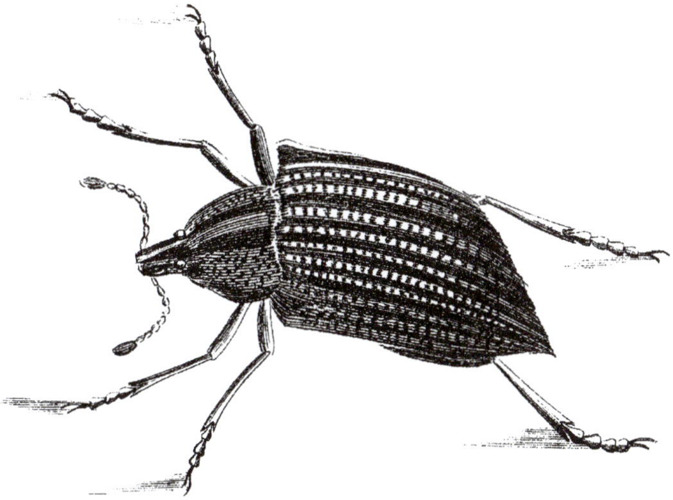

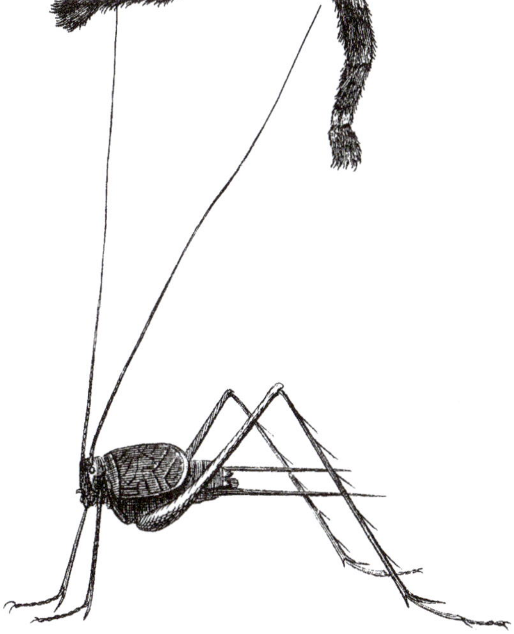

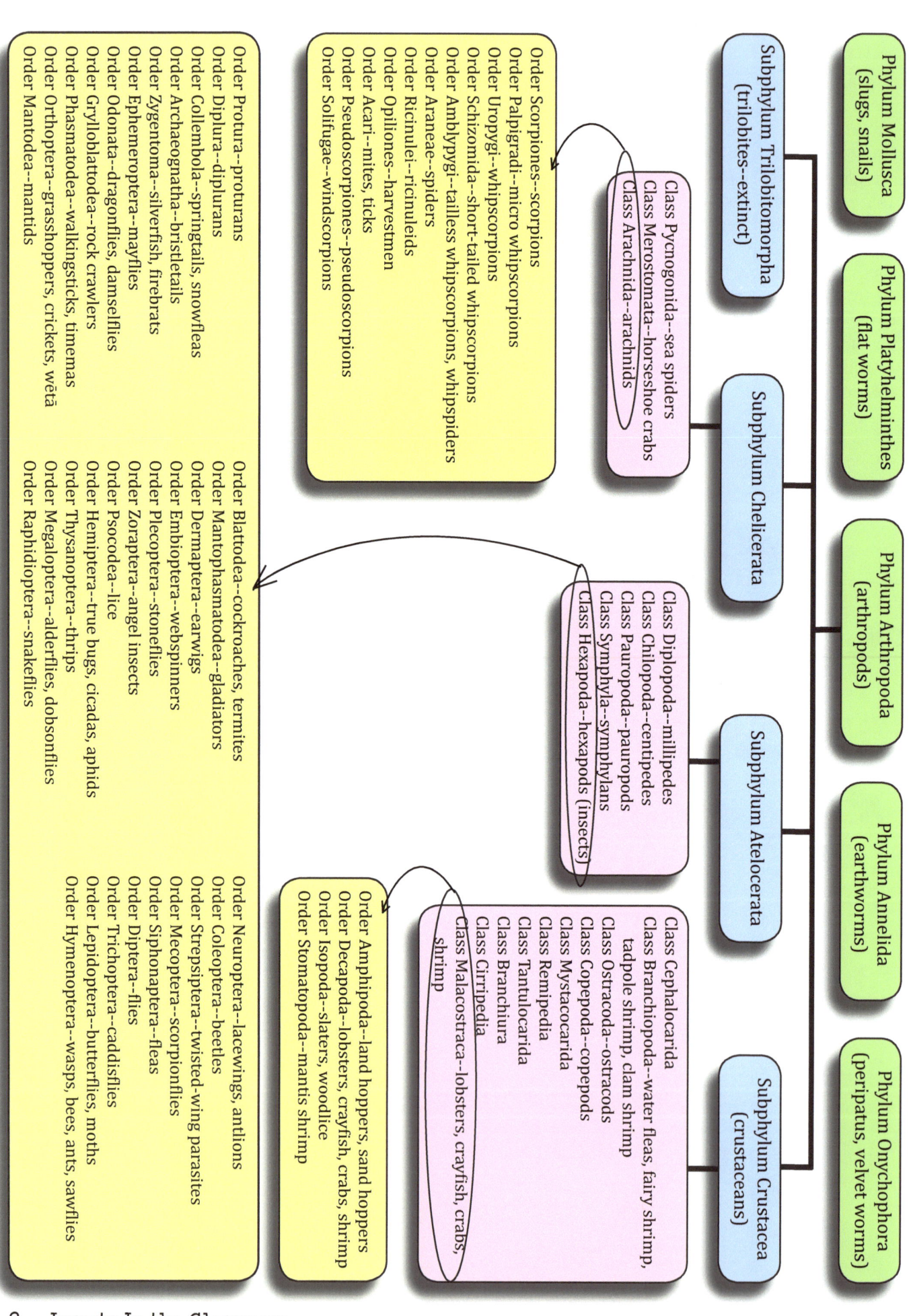

Insects in the Classroom—Why Insects?

Presumably, you have picked up this book because you already have an interest in insects. However, if you are trying to convince your colleagues or supervisor that insects are a valuable addition to the classroom, here are a few points to ponder.

Cost and Availability

Want to bring wildlife into the classroom? Want your students to be able to see nature red in tooth and claw? Too bad a pride of lions doesn't fit in the classroom, and those wolves are so expensive to feed.

Insects are free. You and your students can collect them outdoors, even in the most urban of settings. They generally require little space or equipment to keep in the classroom. A jam jar or ice cream container is all that is needed to house many insects, and relatively inexpensive plastic aquaria can be purchased at most pet stores. If you can't be bothered to collect insects, or if you want large quantities, you can purchase them at modest prices from live insect suppliers. (See the Resources section on page 66.)

Time

Insects require little maintenance. Unlike a rabbit, guinea pig, or parakeet, insects do not generally need daily care. Even the most needy insects can usually get by with attention two or three times a week, and with the proper set-up some can be ignored for a month with no problem.

Importance to Humans

Insects matter. Without them we humans (and most other vertebrates) couldn't survive. Here are just a few of the ways insects are important to us.

Natural Ecology

Insects are essential components of terrestrial ecosystems. They perform roles as pollinators, decomposers, predators, and prey. Their sheer numbers reflect their importance in natural systems. There are nearly a million species of insect described by scientists, and up to 7.8 million as yet undiscovered species (compare that with about 4,000 mammalian species). There are an estimated 200 million insects per person on earth. And lest you think that because they're small their numbers don't amount to much, one study found that a third of the animal biomass in the Amazon rainforest is made up of just ants and termites.

Agriculture

Human agriculture is intimately linked with insects. Pest insects threaten crops and livestock; beneficial insects help keep pests and weeds in check; and bees and other insects pollinate fruits and vegetables. According to Apiculture New Zealand, the value of honeybees alone in New Zealand is over $3 billion annually. This includes the $48.2 million per year beekeeping industry, pollination of pasture legumes, and crop pollination. If insects were to suddenly vanish, much of our food and fibre production would vanish along with them.

Food

In most human societies, insects provide an important source of nutrition. High in protein and essential nutrients like iron and calcium, insects provide up to 10% of the animal protein in some people's diets. In New Zealand today, **entomophagy** (insect eating) is generally limited to a novelty at the Wild Foods Festival and at some restaurants. The traditional Māori diet, however, included a variety of insects, some of which are considered pests today.

Though New Zealanders don't often knowingly eat insects today, there are plenty of insects and insect-derived products on the supermarket shelves. Honey is the obvious one, but there are others.

The red food dye, carmine, also known as cochineal, is sold as a food colouring and is used in a variety of products, from fruit juice to candy to cosmetics. This dye is made from the bodies of the cochineal scale insect (*Dactylopius coccus*).

Another insect product in our food is shellac. Shellac is produced by the lac insect, *Laccifer lacca*. It is used to add gloss to candies and fresh fruit. It is also used as a wood and leather finish, as a coating on pills, as a dye, in printer ink, in cosmetics, and in a wide range of other manufactured goods.

Medicine

Insects and their products have been used in folk medicine for centuries. Even in today's modern medicine, insects have a place. Blow fly larvae are sometimes employed to clean wounds, as they eat only dead flesh, and excrete allantoin, which promotes healing, leaving a wound clean and better able to heal. Honey's antimicrobial properties are also used to help heal wounds. Honey and beeswax are used to treat a variety of skin disorders. Bee and ant venom are used to treat arthritis. Beeswax has been used to create slow-release drug capsules. Extracts from blister beetles have shown promise against cancer in the laboratory, and more insect products are tested every day for medicinal properties.

Silk

About 32 million kilograms of silk are produced each year and are woven into high-value textiles. Silk is produced by the caterpillar of the moth *Bombyx mori*.

Fascination

Anyone who works with children knows that many children are fascinated by insects. Almost everyone has an emotional response to insects. We may love them. We may hate them. We may be terrified of them. But we respond to them on a gut level. Teachers can use this visceral response to engage students in the subject of insects.

Flexibility

Art, maths, science, English, social studies… insects lend themselves to nearly any subject. Use them as an excuse to get your students outside, or bring insects into the classroom for a rainy-day activity. Raucous games, quiet reflection, scientific investigation…you can do it all with insects.

Inviting Insects Onto the School Grounds

Planting an insect garden is a great way to invite arthropods to school. I use the term "insect" for simplicity, but a good "insect" garden will attract spiders, centipedes, millipedes, and slaters as well.

Like all animals, insects need food, water, and shelter to survive. An insect garden must provide all these things in order to attract insects.

Food

Flowering plants for nectar and pollen—Many insects eat nectar or pollen as adults. Providing year-round flowers of the right type will attract a wide variety of flies, butterflies, beetles, beneficial wasps, and bees to the garden. Choose plants with small, flat, open flowers, which provide the best access to nectar. Choose a mix of plants so that you have year-round flowers.

Some particularly good insect-attracting flowers are:
- Coriander
- Dill
- Fennel
- Mint
- Lemon balm
- Monarda (bee balm, bergamot)
- Oregano
- Rosemary
- Sunflowers
- Scabiosa
- Daisies
- Yarrow
- Cosmos
- Chamomile

Food for predatory insects—Students can see some exciting predator/prey interactions if your garden provides abundant food for predators. Plant lettuces, cabbage and broccoli to encourage aphids, white butterfly caterpillars, and slugs that will attract a variety of predators and parasites.

Water

Though many insects get the water they need from their food, some appreciate a shallow dish of water with a wide lip, or a small puddle, particularly on hot dry days.

Shelter

Encourage insects to settle down and reproduce in your garden by providing adequate shelter from predators and the elements. Shelter should include:

- Logs, rocks, overturned flowerpots, or stacks of bricks.
- Plants of varied heights, including some dense groundcovers.
- Shady spots.

Other Attractants

Sunning spots—Many insects like sunny places for warming up in the morning. Set a large rock in a sunny spot or incorporate a sunny wall of the building into your insect garden.

Puddling spots—A puddle or patch of mud can attract butterflies who "puddle", sucking up the mineral-laden moisture from the soil.

Mānuka and kānuka—If stick insects are present in your neighbourhood, mānuka and kānuka can attract them to your school grounds.

Ake ake—This tree is frequented by katydids, which can be found by listening for their late afternoon "zit!" call.

Long grass—Crickets prefer long grass and will set up house in an unmowed corner of the school grounds.

Swan plant—This plant will attract monarch butterflies, as it is the only food plant for their caterpillars. Be aware, however, that the plant is poisonous.

Caring for Insects in the Classroom

Mealworm

Mealworms can be purchased from pet shops and live insect suppliers. To culture mealworms, put 5 to 10 cm of wheat bran in the bottom of a plastic pan. Add 25 to 50 beetles, and place a small slice of potato on top of the meal for moisture.

The beetles start laying eggs 7 to 10 days after emergence, and the eggs hatch about 14 days later. The time spent in the larval stage varies considerably with temperature and food availability. The larvae grow rapidly under ideal conditions until they are about 25 mm long, then they pupate. The adults emerge 2 to 3 weeks after pupation.

Slater

Slaters can be collected from moist garden areas. There are two easily distinguishable groups of slaters—those that can curl into a hard ball (in the family Armadillidae), and those that can't curl up (in the families Oniscidae and Porcellionidae). Females of both groups carry eggs in a brood pouch. Development from young to adult usually takes about a year.

Slaters should be placed in a container (large jar, aquarium, bucket, or deep tray) with 2-3 cm of soil on the bottom. The soil should be kept moist, but not wet. Small pieces of wood can be added for the slaters to hide under. Feed them slices of potato and dead leaves.

Praying Mantis

New Zealand praying mantis eggs are deposited on branches, tree trunks, fence posts, and walls in the fall in a greyish foam case with a white "plait" down the front. The egg case overwinters, and the young hatch in the spring and mature through summer.

Each egg case contains up to 70 eggs. Collect egg cases in late winter by clipping the branch to which they are attached and placing it in an aquarium or jar. Observe the eggs daily to watch for emerging mantids.

Praying mantids are cannibalistic and must be housed individually or in a very large aquarium with lots of vegetation so the mantids can hide from one another. A small jar can be used for young mantids. A thin cloth secured with an elastic band makes a good lid, and a small stick will provide a roost for the young insect.

Praying mantids must be fed live insects. Fruit flies and aphids are excellent foods for young mantids. As the mantids grow, provide larger food (house flies and blow flies are good). Provide water by misting the cage every day or two.

Monarch Butterfly

Monarchs can be kept year round in the classroom. Collect caterpillars during the summer. Caterpillars can be kept on potted swan plants or cut swan plant branches in the classroom. The plants need not be in a cage. To keep caterpillars from wandering, place the pot in a tray of water—the caterpillars will not cross the water.

As caterpillars pupate and emerge as adults, transfer them to a large cage. Feed them fresh flowers or a 20% sugar solution, refreshed daily. To feed sugar solution, place a small piece of sponge or a folded paper towel in a jar lid and soak with sugar solution.

Adults will lay small yellowish eggs on swan plants placed in the cage. You will need to have several potted swan plants growing in the classroom to use as food for the emerging larvae. As the eggs hatch and the larvae grow, monitor the population carefully and cull caterpillars as needed so that they do not strip all your swan plants (kill excess caterpillars by placing in a container in the freezer). If you run out of swan plants, you can rear caterpillars on slices of fresh pumpkin. Pumpkin is not a natural food for monarchs, and caterpillars cannot complete their entire development on it—expect young ones to die. Older caterpillars will be able to complete their development, however.

Activities/Lessons

Each activity includes a quick-reference icon at the top right corner of the page--

 = indoor activities

 = outdoor activities

What is an Insect?

Insects have many features in common.

Summary

Students observe insects and record their features.

Learning Objectives

Students will:
1) Observe and describe the features all insects have in common.
2) Observe and discuss the importance of adaptations.

Curriculum Connections

Science, Living World, Life Processes

Vocabulary

head, thorax, abdomen, antenna, compound eye, adaptation

Materials

Live insects (1 per pair of students)
Clear jars or other containers for the insects
Whiteboard, blackboard, or large piece of paper

Time

15-30 minutes

Age

Years 0-6

Group size

Any

Introduction/Set-up

Collect a variety of insects—one for every two students in the class. Put the insects into clear containers so they can be observed. Make sure the insects are large enough that students can see the features on them. They should be able to count legs and antennae, and see wings, eyes, and body divisions.

Activity

Divide the students into pairs and give each pair an insect. Give the students several minutes to observe their insects. Older students should write down things they notice about their insects. Younger students can simply observe.

Have students share their observations. Record the observations on the whiteboard or on a large piece of butcher paper. If groups come up with the same observations, put a tick or a number by that observation to show how many groups saw it.

Conclusion

Discuss the students' observations, beginning with those that are common to all insects. Common insect features the students may have observed include:

- Six legs
- Two antennae
- Three main body parts (head, thorax, and abdomen)
- Wings (not all insects have wings, but insects are the only arthropods with wings, so it's a distinguishing feature)
- Compound eyes

Circle these observations on the board. Ask the groups to confirm that their insects have these features.

Now discuss with students the other observations. All their insects had common features. Did they all look the same? No. Each species of insect has unique features. Many of these features are adaptations that help an insect survive in its habitat. Discuss some of the unique observations the students made, and how those features might be adaptations (e.g. a brown insect might be well-camouflaged, an insect with big back legs might be good at jumping away from its enemies, an insect with long antennae might be good at feeling its way around in the dark).

Extensions

1. Have students research a particular insect of their choice. Once they've learned about their insect, have them draw a picture of the insect, labelling those features common to all insects, and also labelling features that are adaptations that help their insect survive.

2. Have students invent their own insects. Their insects should have all the features common to insects. They should also give their insects some special adaptations. Younger students might simply draw their insects and share them verbally with the class. Older students could create posters that describe the features of their insects.

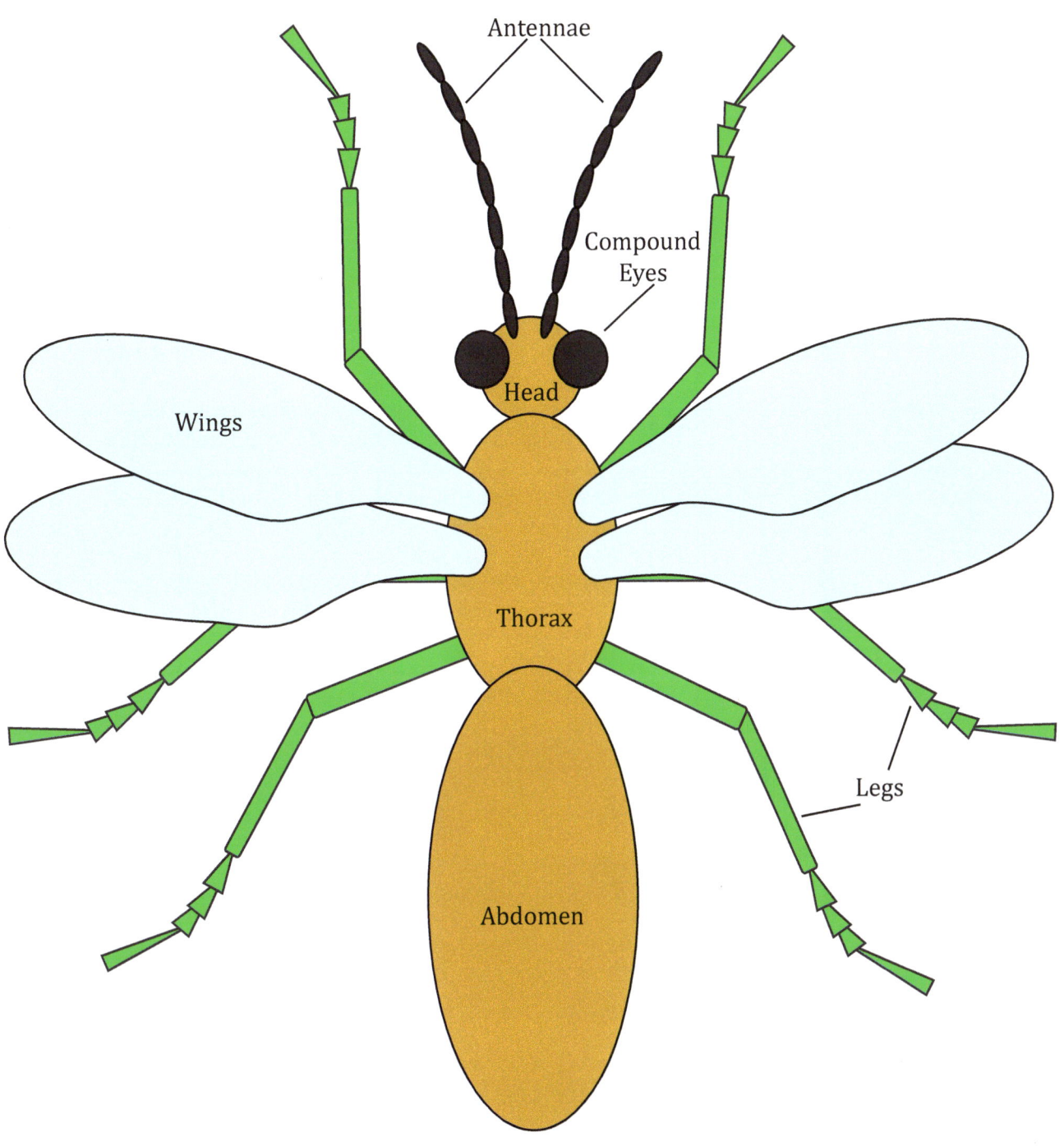

Insects In the Classroom

Insect/Spider Puzzles

Head, thorax, abdomen...insects and spiders have many parts.

Summary

Students put together insect and spider puzzles.

Learning Objectives

Students will:
1) Describe how insect and spider bodies are the same and different

Curriculum Connections

Science, Living World, Life Processes

Vocabulary

head, thorax, abdomen, antenna, cephalothorax, spinneret, pedipalp

Materials

Insect and spider puzzle pieces (1 set for each group)
Live insects and spiders or photos
Whiteboard, blackboard, or large piece of paper

Time

15-30 minutes

Age

Years 0-6

Group size

Any

Introduction/Set-up

Copy and cut out insect and spider puzzles—one of each for every three students.

Activity

Working in groups of no more than three, have students assemble each puzzle as they think it should be assembled.

Once groups have completed their puzzles, give them a live insect and live spider, or photos of each. Ask them to carefully observe the animals, then change their puzzles if they need to.

Conclusion

As a whole group, discuss how students assembled their puzzles. Draw an example of an insect and a spider on the whiteboard, putting legs, antennae, and other body parts in the right places. Discuss the name, function, and location of each part of the body. Discuss differences and similarities between insect and spider bodies.

Insect

Spider

16 Insects In the Classroom

Insect Puzzle
Cut out each piece and assemble into an insect.

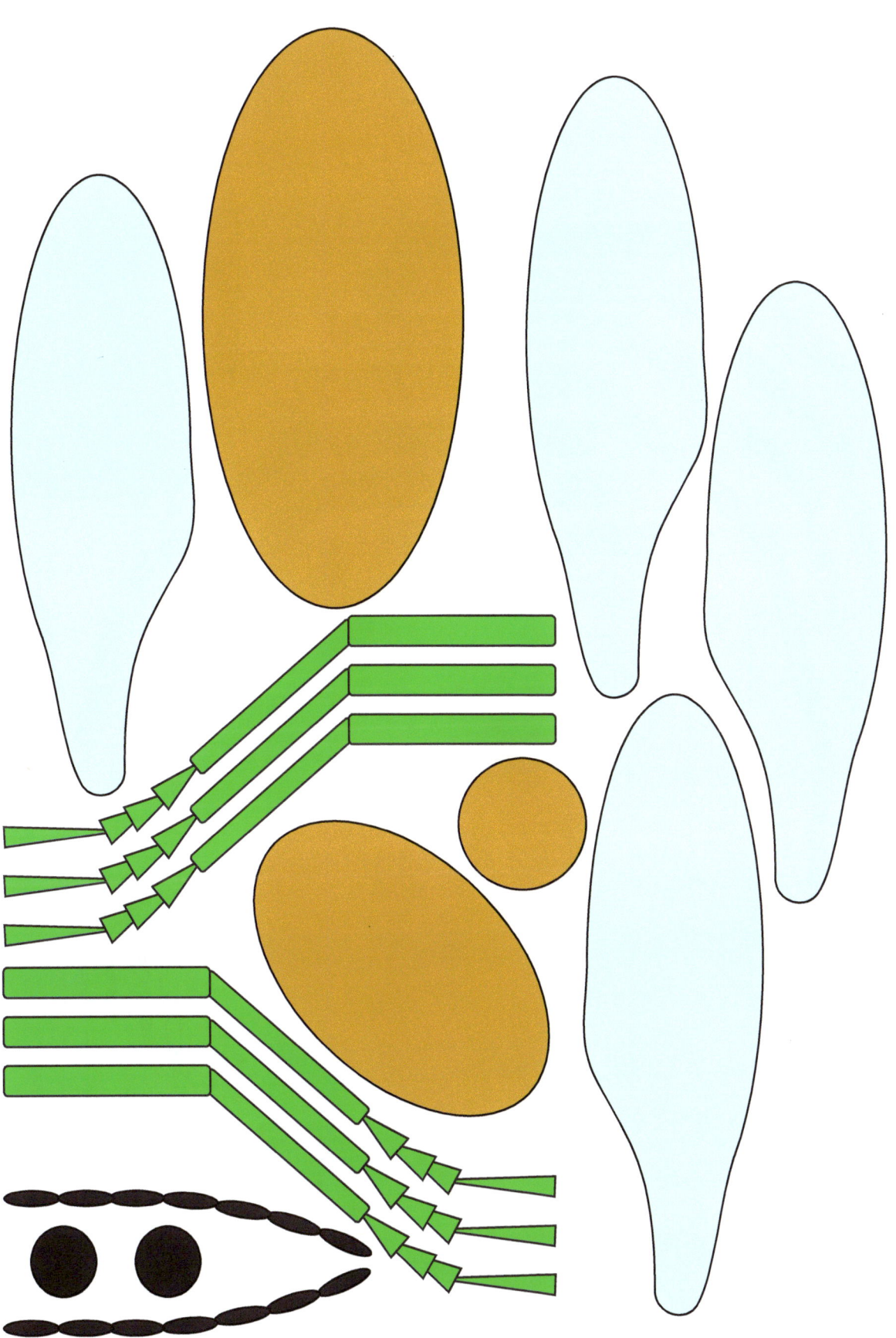

Insects In the Classroom 17

Spider Puzzle
Cut out each piece and assemble into a spider.

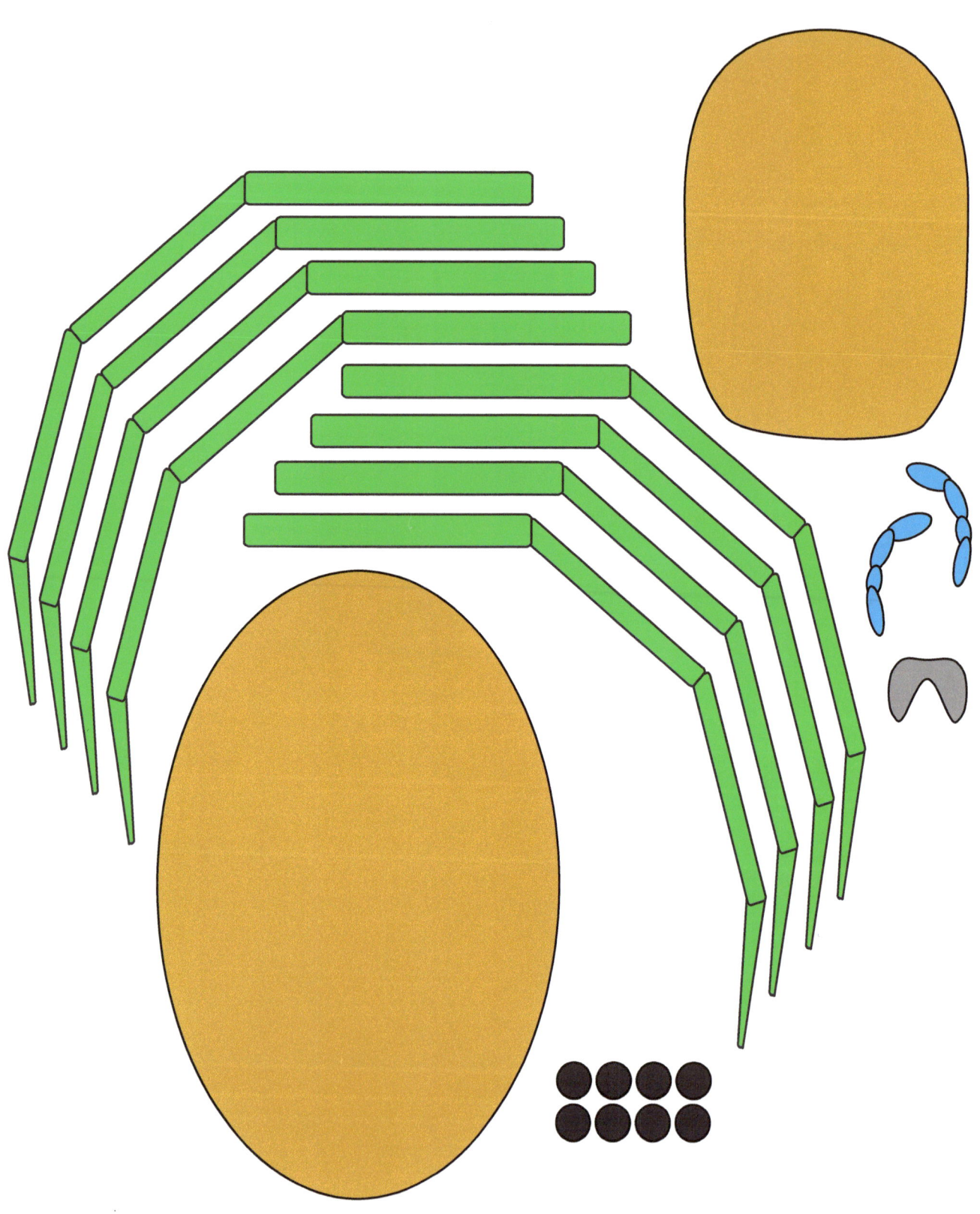

18   Insects In the Classroom

Parts of an Insect

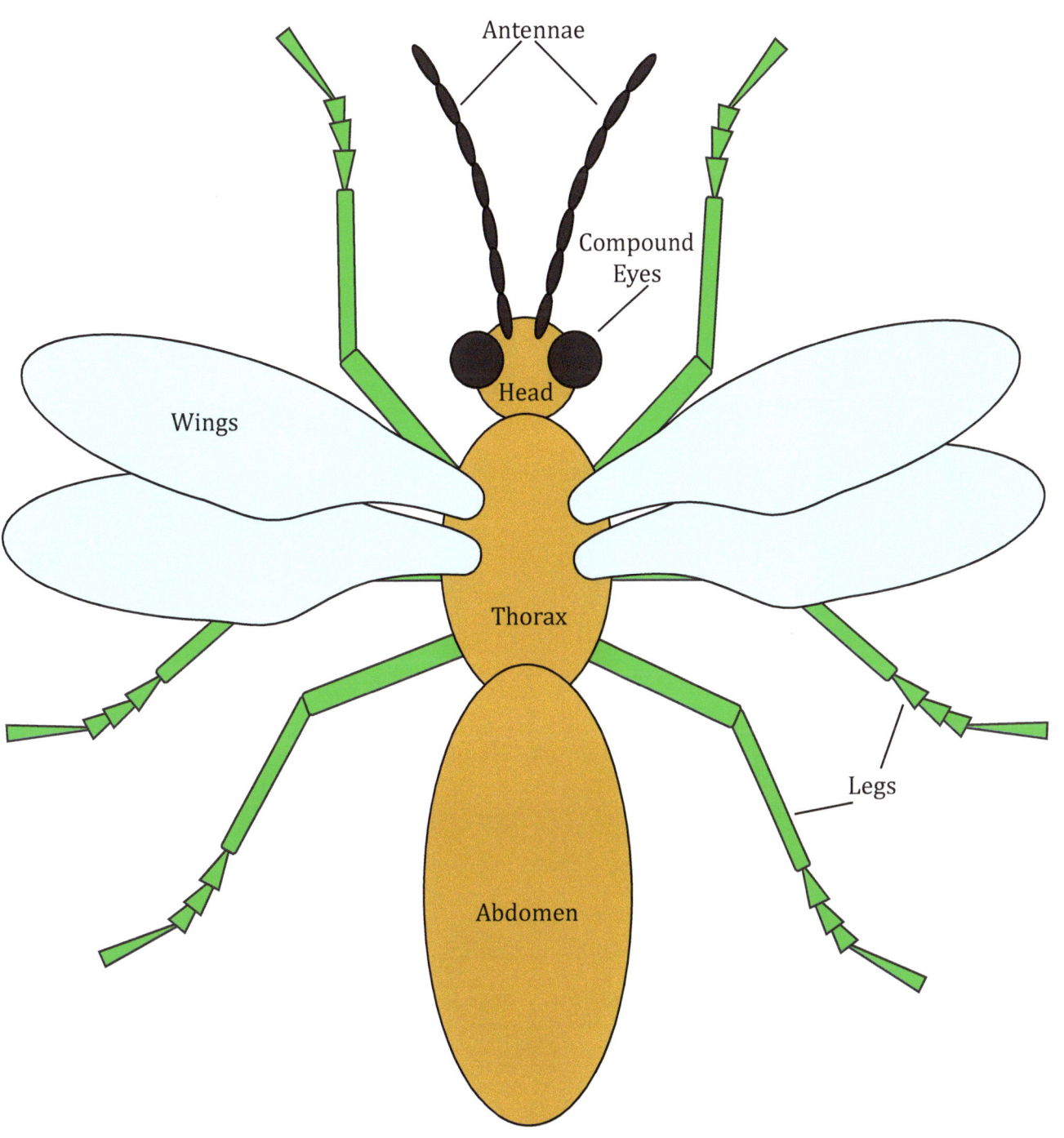

Insects In the Classroom

Parts of a Spider

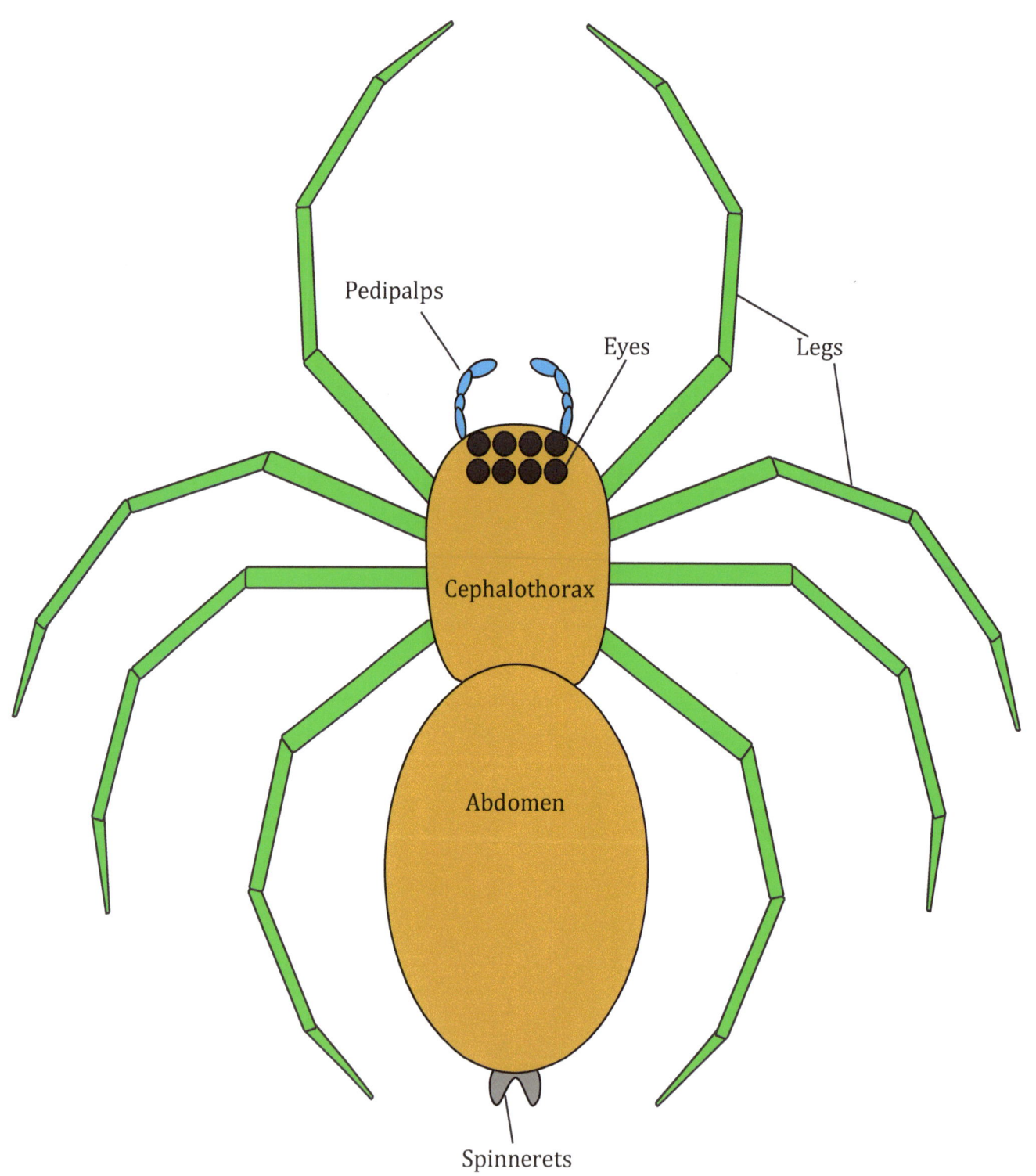

Camouflage Game

Many insects hide by blending in with their habitat.

Summary

Students search for multi-coloured pipe cleaners hidden in a natural environment.

Learning Objectives

Students will:
1) Explain the concept of camouflage.
2) Name colours that would serve as camouflage in a particular habitat.

Curriculum Connections

Science, Living World, Ecology
Science, Living World, Evolution

Vocabulary

camouflage, habitat, evolution, natural selection

Materials

Multi-coloured pipe cleaners (equal numbers of several colours including red, yellow, orange, black, green, and brown; 3-4 per student)
Boundary markers

Time

15-30 minutes

Age

Years 0-6

Group size

Any

Introduction/Set-up

Place pipe cleaners (three to four per student) in a natural area (a wooded area is best, but tall grass works, too). You can simply scatter the pipe cleaners over the ground, but the game is more challenging and realistic if you wind pipe cleaners around tree branches, wedge them in bark, or place them partly concealed under rocks, logs or leaves. All pipe cleaners should be at least partly visible without moving anything.

Discuss insect tactics for avoiding predators (flying, running, burrowing, camouflage, warning colours, stings, etc.). Explain that students will be playing a game to illustrate one of these tactics.

Activity

Explain to students that there are pipe cleaners hidden within the boundary markers. On a signal from the teacher, students should enter the playing area, collect just one pipe cleaner, and return to the start. Record the number of each colour of pipe cleaner collected. Send students back into the playing field, this time for two minutes. Students should collect as many pipe cleaners as they can find in this time.

Conclusion

Discuss the number of pipe cleaners of each colour collected. Explain that there were equal numbers of each colour placed in the playing area. Why were more red, orange, and yellow pipe cleaners collected in the first round? How did those numbers change in the second round? Why? If you were an insect, what colour would you rather be? Why? Were there other factors that made a pipe cleaner difficult to find (e.g. where it was placed or how it was shaped)? Does camouflage depend entirely on colour?

If all pipe cleaners have not been collected, send students back to finish collecting them.

A good follow-up to this activity is to have students search for real insects in the same area. Ask students: What colours are the real insects? Where did you have to look for them? Was it easy or difficult to find them? What strategies other than camouflage do the insects you found use for defence?

Extension

Give students pipe cleaners to create their own insects. Have them hide them outdoors for other students to find. Discuss what features made the insects easier or more difficult to find.

With older students, discuss the process of **natural selection** that caused camouflage to **evolve** in so many different insects (Insects that are better at hiding survive and produce offspring that look like them). A good example of this **evolution** in action is the case of the peppered moth (*Biston betularia*). Before the industrial revolution, the peppered moth was light coloured, with small black spots—perfectly camouflaged on light coloured tree trunks. In the mid-1800s, pollution from new, coal-powered industries darkened tree trunks around London, England with soot. The light coloured moths now stood out clearly on the tree trunks, and were easily picked off by birds. Only the rare darkly coloured moths survived to reproduce, leading to the rapid evolution of dark colouration in the moths. Within 35 years, nearly all peppered moths between London and Manchester were dark coloured.

Assessment

Have students invent an imaginary insect that lives in the classroom and uses camouflage for defence. What colours would it be? What shape? Where would it hide? How would it behave in order to stay hidden?

Chemical Warfare

Insects use bright colours to tell predators they are poisonous.

Summary

Students play the roles of predator and toxic or non-toxic prey in an active game of tag.

Learning Objectives

Students will:
1) Explain the concept of warning colouration.
2) Name three colours or colour combinations that insects use as warning colouration.

Curriculum Connections

Science, Living World, Ecology
Science, Living World, Evolution

Vocabulary

warning colouration, aposematic colouration, predator, prey

Materials

Red and green bandannas or strips of cloth (enough of each colour for half the students)
Markers for the playing field
Whiteboard or newsprint on an easel

Time

15-30 minutes

Age

Years 4-6

Group size

Any

Introduction/Set-up

Mark the boundaries of the playing field. Give plenty of room for students to run.

Tell students they are going to play a predator-prey game. Do not reveal the nature of the game.

Activity

Designate three students as predators and the rest as prey. Hand out bandannas to the prey (equal numbers of each colour). Do not indicate any significance of colour. Prey should tuck their bandannas in their back pockets or in the back of their trousers with a long tail sticking out. Explain that the predators are trying to score as many points as they can by collecting bandannas from the prey. When a prey's bandanna is removed he/she should step to the side of the playing field until the end of the round. Keep the round short—do not allow all the prey to be caught.

At the end of the first round of play, count the number of each colour of bandanna the predators caught. Write these numbers on the whiteboard, and explain that the green "prey" are worth one point each, but the red "prey" are poisonous, and are worth negative one point. Calculate the predators' score and write it on the board.

Play another round, challenging the predators to improve their score.

Conclusion

Discuss why there were fewer red bandannas caught during the second round. Why did predators avoid them? Explain that, just like in the game, if a prey insect is poisonous, it may still be eaten if the predators don't know it is poisonous. Poisonous insects often advertise their poison by being brightly coloured (e.g. ladybugs, monarch butterflies, bees and wasps). Predators learn to avoid these brightly coloured insects.

Discuss how people use warning colouration on road and hazard signs. We use red, orange and yellow, combined with black, just as insects do.

Habitat Mural

Insects live in a variety of habitats, and each habitat contains a unique mix of insects.

Summary

Students create models of insects seen outdoors (or researched) and place them in the correct habitat on a mural.

Learning Objectives

Students will:
1) Explain the concept of habitat.
2) Name at least one insect living in each habitat included in the mural.
3) Describe how the insect they create is adapted for its habitat.

Curriculum Connections

Science, Living World, Ecology
Science, Living World, Evolution

Vocabulary

habitat, adaptation

Materials

- 5-6 metre length of butcher paper with various habitats drawn onto it (e.g. forest, field, lake, stream)
- Miscellaneous art materials such as egg cartons, pipe cleaners, Styrofoam balls, felt, fabric, beads, coloured paper, etc.
- Glue and tape
- Felts, crayons, or coloured pencils
- Scissors

Time: 1-2 hours field trip, 30-60 minutes in the classroom

Age: Years 0-6

Group size: Any

Introduction/Set-up

A habitat mural is a great way to get kids to think about the insects they've seen outdoors and what habitats different insects live in.

On a 5-6 metre long piece of butcher paper, draw and label the various habitats students may have experience with (forest, field, lake, stream, beach). Hang this paper on the wall, securing it well so that it does not fall with the weight of the insects the students will attach to it.

Activity

If you can, visit various habitats in the community and have the students search for insects. If it is not possible to visit and see insects in person, you can have the students research insect habitats on the internet or in the library.

Provide the students ample art materials and ask them to create (as accurately as possible) insects they have seen (or researched) in each of the habitats on the mural. Students then attach their insects in the appropriate habitat.

Conclusion

Discuss how each insect is adapted for its particular habitat.

Extension

Have students draw other organisms that live in each habitat on the mural (fish, birds, mammals, reptiles, amphibians, other invertebrates, etc.). Discuss the various interactions among organisms in any environment (predator-prey interactions, competition, mutualisms, symbioses). Draw lines between organisms that interact in some way. Discuss the complex web of interconnections, and how those connections make the task of understanding and managing the natural world difficult.

Invertebrate Survey

Invertebrates can be found in many habitats, and each type of invertebrate has its own niche.

Summary

Students collect invertebrates in their habitats by closely observing a small area.

Learning Objectives

Students will:
1) Explain the concepts of habitat and niche.
2) Be able to find insects outdoors.

Curriculum Connections

Science, Living World, Ecology
Science, Living World, Evolution
Science, Nature of Science,
　　Understanding about Science
　　Investigating in Science
　　Participating and Contributing

Vocabulary

habitat, niche, sample

Materials

Magnifying lenses (1 per pair of students)
String circles (approx. 1 m diameter; 1 per pair of students)
Trowels (1 per pair of students)
Jars or collecting containers (3 per pair of students)
Arthropod identification sheets (see Identifying Insects, p 59)

Time: 1 hour

Age: Years 4-6

Group size: Any

Introduction/Set-up

Choose a site for the students to study. A park with a forested area, or long grass are good locations.

When scientists study nature, they often take a sample—they look at a small portion of the community and assume that the rest is similar. Explain to the students that they are going to look at a sample of the park's invertebrate community, and record the organisms that live in different niches in the park.

Activity

Pair the students and give each pair a magnifying lens, string circle, trowel, 3 collecting jars, and an identification sheet. Give the students the following instructions:

1. Place your string on the ground, creating a circle. Inside the string is your study site. You will look for insects only inside the circle.
2. First, observe the insects and other arthropods you can see in the undisturbed plants. Record features of these animals—colours, sizes, movement, behaviour, etc. Collect at least one animal from this layer.
3. Next, look carefully through the leaf litter or thatch for insects or other arthropods. Again, record features of these animals. Collect at least one animal from this layer.
4. Finally, dig into the soil. Record what you find, and collect at least one animal from this layer.

Conclusion

When students have finished collecting, ask them to place their jars of invertebrates into three groups based on what "layer" the animals came from—plants, leaf litter/thatch, or soil. Ask students to look at the collections of animals. Were different animals found in different places? Discuss the fact that each animal has different habitat needs and roles within the ecosystem, so we find them in different places. Use some of the collected animals as examples to illustrate this (e.g. you may choose a worm and note that it lives in the soil, where it finds dead leaves to eat, moisture, and protection from birds). Be sure to release all organisms when you are done.

Insect Classification

Insects are grouped by scientists based on common features.

Summary

Students group insects based on features they can see, then compare their groupings with scientific ones.

Learning Objectives

Students will:
1) Explain how scientists classify insects.

Curriculum Connections

Science, Living World, Evolution
Science, Nature of Science, Understanding about Science

Vocabulary

classification, phylogeny, order

Materials

Copies of insect photos—1 set of 12 for every pair of students
Paper and pencils
Insect identification key (optional, see Identifying Insects, page 59)

Time

30-50 minutes

Age

Years 4-6

Group size

Any

Introduction/Set-up

Copy and cut out the insect photos on the following page. You'll need one set of 12 photos for every pair of students.

Activity

Begin with a prior lesson or discussion on insect features—those features they have in common and those that are unique to each species. Discuss the fact that scientists use these similarities and differences to classify, or group, insects so they can understand them better.

Divide students into pairs. Give each pair a set of insect photos, paper, and a pencil.

Ask students to look at the insects and group (classify) them in any way they would like, based on the features they can see. Tell them not to worry about "identifying" the insects—the point is to simply observe and use those observations to guide their classification. Tell students they should aim for two to four groups of insects. On the paper, they should write down which insects are in each group, and what features they used to define each of the groups.

When students have completed classifying their insects, ask each group to share what their classification scheme was. You will find that students have used a variety of criteria. Explain that the process students have just gone through is the same type of process scientists use to classify insects—looking at the insects' features to try to determine which ones are more closely related (i.e. have more features in common). Scientists also use DNA to help with classification, but the same principle applies—the more they have in common, the more closely related they are.

Using an identification key, have students try to key out each of the insects to determine what order scientists place them in. Orders are broad groups, and the features defining the order are usually easily seen without magnification.

Discuss the groups scientists use. Are they the same or different from the ones in which students placed the insects? If students have trouble identifying the insects, the answers are listed below.

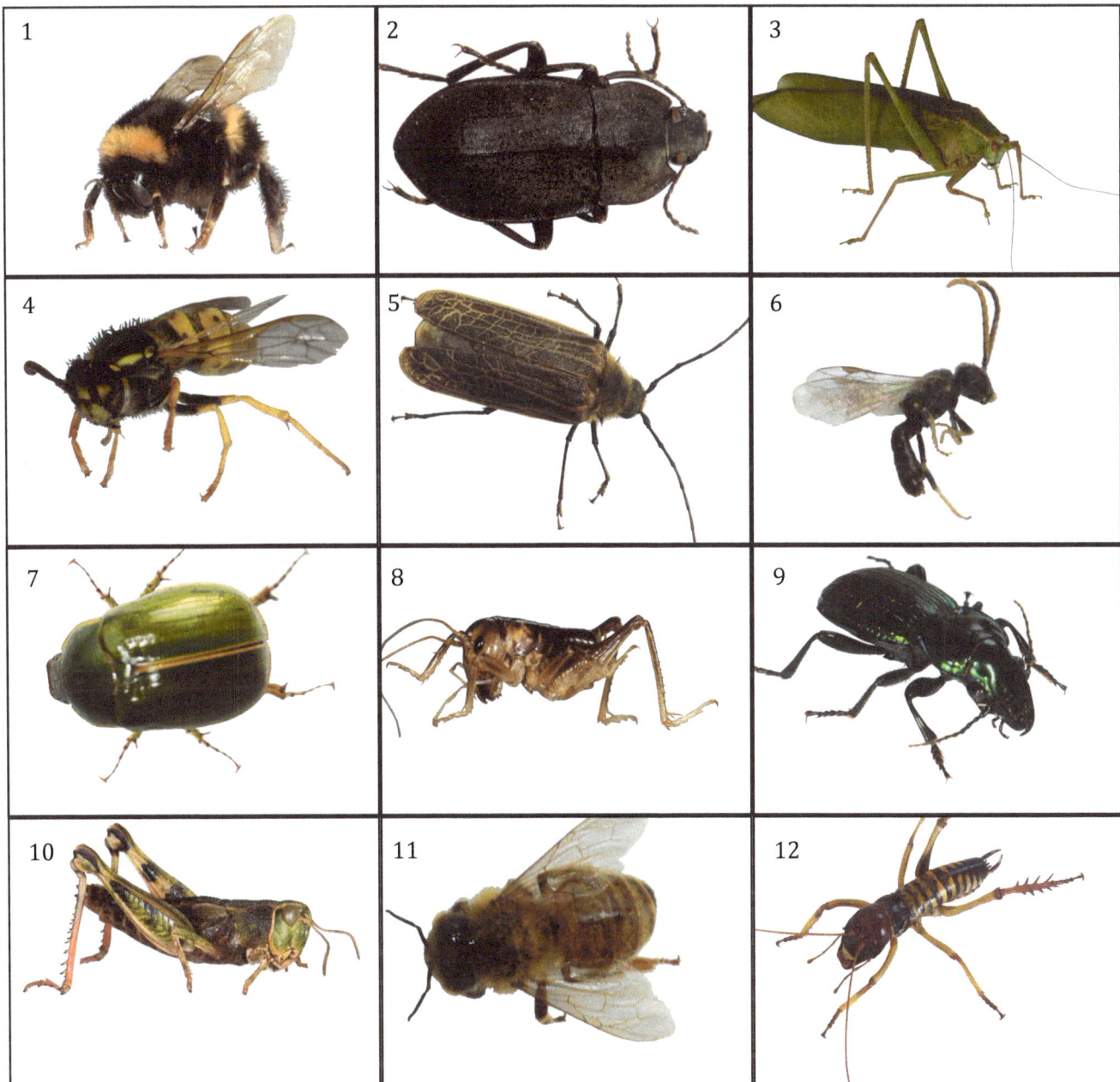

How do scientists classify these insects?

Hymenoptera—bees, wasps, ants
    1. Bumble bee
    4. German wasp
    6. Native bee
    11. Honey bee

Coleoptera—beetles
    2. False wireworm
    5. Huhu beetle
    7. Tanguru chafer
    9. Metallic green ground beetle

Orthoptera—grasshoppers, crickets, wētā
    3. Katydid
    8. Ground wētā
    10. Southern tussock grasshopper
    12. Wellington tree wētā

Insects In the Classroom

Honey Bee Dance

Honey bees dance to tell others where the best nectar is.

Summary

Students play the role of foraging honey bees, searching for hidden "flowers" by interpreting a dance.

Learning Objectives

Students will:
1) Describe how bees communicate the location of flowers.

Curriculum Connections

Science, Living World, Life Processes

Vocabulary

communication, social insects

Materials

Toy, ball or other small object representing a patch of flowers

Time

15 minutes

Age

Years 0-6

Group size

4-30

Introduction/Set-up

Honey bees use a "dance" to tell other members of the hive where to find flowers. The honey bee dance communicates the direction and distance other bees should fly in order get to the flowers. Smells and tastes on the scout bee provide additional clues. This game is a great component of or follow-up to a lesson on honey bees, or a visit by a local beekeeper.

Activity

Form students into a circle. This is the "hive." One student plays the role of the scout. Everyone else stays in the hive, covers their eyes, and sings loudly (any song—the idea is to make noise so students cannot hear where the scout bee is going). Meanwhile, the scout hides an object representing a patch of flowers. Upon her return, the scout must tell the other students where the hidden object is by performing a bee dance in the centre of the circle.

The dance goes as follows: the scout first runs in a figure eight twice. The axis of the figure eight should point toward the hidden object. Then the scout stops, points her bottom toward the object, and wiggles it once for every metre between the hive and the object. The rest of the bees search for the object, using the scout's dance to guide them. The first student to find the flowers becomes the scout in the next round.

Conclusion

Ask students if they found the dance easy or difficult to interpret. How important was it for the scout to give clear directions? How did students find the flowers even when the scout's directions were unclear? Do you think honey bees do the same thing?

Extension

The real honey bee dance is more complicated than this simple game implies. Students can research the details to learn how the bees' dance changes with the distance of the flowers from the hive, and how bees use the angle of the sun to calculate the direction indicated by the dance. An interactive tutorial of the honey bee dance can be found here: https://content.ces.ncsu.edu/honey-bee-dance-language.

My Favourite Food Is...

Just like people, arthropods have favourite foods.

Summary

Students perform food preference experiments with mealworm beetles and slaters.

Learning Objectives

Students will:
1) Perform a simple experiment.
2) Develop and evaluate a hypothesis.
3) Discuss how their experiment could be improved.

Curriculum Connections

Science, Living World, Life Processes
Science, Nature of Science,
    Understanding about Science
    Investigating in Science
    Participating and Contributing

Vocabulary

preference, trial, hypothesis

Materials

Copies of instruction sheets
Potato and apple slices (2 each per group)
Mealworm beetles and slaters (5-10 per group; See Resource section for suppliers)
Small trays or ice cream tubs (1 per group)

Time: 1 hr

Age: Years 4-6

Group size: Any

Introduction/Set-up

This is a great experiment to do before setting up a colony of mealworms or slaters in the classroom. Though mealworms and slaters have very different habitat requirements, both are often given potato or apple in captivity. For mealworms, the fresh food provides the only source of moisture. For slaters, the fresh food is more of a treat than a necessity (see Caring for Insects in the Classroom, page 12).

Gather materials. Copy instruction and data sheets.

Activity

Explain to the students that they are going to conduct a pair of experiments to find out what foods mealworm beetles and slaters prefer. Briefly explain the experimental set-up and procedure. Remind students that before they do anything, they need to write down their hypothesis—what they think will happen.

Divide students into groups of three. Provide each group with instructions and data sheets, a tray, live organisms, and potato and apple slices. Circulate around the classroom as students set up and start their experiments, ensuring that all the students understand what they are doing.

Conclusion

Have each group present their results to the class. Discuss whether the results were the same among groups. Why might they be different? Discuss some of the problems with the experimental design (there are no repeated trials, the organisms may not be hungry or thirsty, the organisms may be under stress and more interested in safety than food). How could you get a more accurate picture of what each organism prefers, using just the data you've collected? (Pool the results from all groups, giving you repeated trials.) How could you improve the experiment to better gauge food preferences? (Leave the food and organisms together for a longer time period, measure the amount of food eaten rather than the behaviour of the animals, starve the animals for a day beforehand so they are hungry, repeat the experiment several days in a row.)

Extension

Allow students to test a variety of foods of their choice, or to design a food preference experiment for a different organism.

Mealworm Food Preference Experiment

Instructions

1. Record your hypothesis

Write down whether you think mealworms prefer apple or potato.

2. Set up your experiment

Place a piece of apple and a piece of potato in your tray. The pieces should be the same size and be placed the same distance from the centre of the tray.

3. Add your insects

Place your insects in the middle of the tray. If you're using adult beetles, gently nudge any beetles that get stuck on their backs so all are on their feet.

4. Record your data

Wait 1 minute, then record on your tally sheet how many mealworms are touching apple, how many are touching potato, and how many are touching neither apple nor potato.

Wait 2 minutes, and again record the number of mealworms touching apple, potato, and neither apple nor potato. Do this a total of 4 times, at 2 minute intervals.

5. Evaluate your data

Add the numbers in each column on your sheet and write the totals at the bottom.

6. Analyse your data

Discuss the following questions as a group:
- Which food did the mealworms prefer? Was your hypothesis correct?
- Why was it important to record the mealworms that weren't attracted to either food?
- Do you think your experiment was a fair test of mealworm food preferences? Why or why not?
- How could you improve your experiment?

Mealworm Food Preference Experiment

Data sheet

Hypothesis: We think mealworms will prefer _____

Observation	Number on potato	Number on apple	Number on neither
1			
2			
3			
4			
Total			

Mealworm Food Preference Experiment

Data sheet

Hypothesis: We think mealworms will prefer _____

Observation	Number on potato	Number on apple	Number on neither
1			
2			
3			
4			
Total			

Slater Food Preference Experiment

Instructions

1. Record your hypothesis

Write down whether you think slaters prefer apple or potato.

2. Set up your experiment

Place a piece of apple and a piece of potato in your tray. The pieces should be the same size and be placed the same distance from the centre of the tray.

3. Add your slaters

Place your slaters in the middle of the tray. Gently nudge any slaters that get stuck on their backs so all are on their feet.

4. Record your data

Wait 1 minute, then record on your tally sheet how many slaters are touching apple, how many are touching potato, and how many are touching neither apple nor potato.

Wait 2 minutes, and again record the number of slaters touching apple, potato, and neither apple nor potato. Do this a total of 4 times, at 2 minute intervals.

5. Evaluate your data

Add the numbers in each column on your sheet and write the totals at the bottom.

6. Analyse your data

Discuss the following questions as a group:
- Which food did the slaters prefer? Was your hypothesis correct?
- Why was it important to record the slaters that weren't attracted to either food?
- Do you think your experiment was a fair test of slater food preferences? Why or why not?
- How could you improve your experiment?

Slater Food Preference Experiment

Data sheet

Hypothesis: We think slaters will prefer _____

Observation	Number on potato	Number on apple	Number on neither
1			
2			
3			
4			
Total			

Slater Food Preference Experiment

Data sheet

Hypothesis: We think slaters will prefer _____

Observation	Number on potato	Number on apple	Number on neither
1			
2			
3			
4			
Total			

Honey Bees In Trouble

Intensified modern agriculture is killing the bees it relies upon to function.

Summary

Students play the role of foraging honey bees and discover how pesticides can harm bees.

Learning Objectives

Students will:
1) Describe bee foraging patterns.
2) Discuss how pesticide use can harm bees.

Curriculum Connections

Science, Living World, Life Processes

Vocabulary

pesticide, forage, pollination, colony collapse disorder

Materials

Coloured tokens (see figure on p. 37)
Chalk or hula hoops to designate hives
Signs for foraging areas (see figure on p. 37)

Time

30 minutes

Age

Years 4-6

Group size

Any

Introduction/Set-up

Set up the playing field and prepare pollen tokens ahead of time as indicated in the figure on page 37.

Begin with a discussion or activities on the importance of honey bees and the dangers that face them.

Humans have a long history with honey bees. People have been harvesting honey from wild bees for at least 3 million years. Intensive harvesting has been done for about 10,000 years, and honey bees were domesticated about 2,500 years ago.

Honey isn't the only benefit we get from honey bees. Today, crop pollination is the main role honey bees play in human affairs. We also get pollen from bees, use honey and bee venom in medicine, and enlist bees as bomb sniffers, among other things.

With all these uses, modern honey bee management is intense.

Eighty-four percent of our crops are pollinated by insects, and honey bees perform about 90% of this pollination. Modern bee keepers move hives from crop to crop, based on the pollination services that are required.

Unfortunately, while this system is good for the crops, it's less than ideal for the bees. In today's agricultural landscapes, where a single crop may cover thousands of hectares and weeds are minimal, a honey bee colony can suffer poor nutrition because of the limited variety in the bees' diet. Not all nectar and pollen are the same, and just as we need a variety of foods to remain healthy, so do bees.

In addition, crops are often heavily sprayed with pesticides and herbicides which can have devastating effects on bees. Even small residues of pesticides can harm bees. The chemicals make their way into the hive in pollen and nectar, and harm young and adults alike.

Poor nutrition and agricultural chemicals make bees more susceptible to parasites and pathogens, which are spread easily when hives are moved from place to place and crowded into agricultural fields to ensure effective pollination.

Insects In the Classroom

The result is a syndrome called **Colony Collapse Disorder** (CCD). In CCD, colonies rapidly lose adult workers—they fly away and never return. In the United States, where CCD is particularly prevalent, up to 90% of colonies can die off each year.

Activity

Explain to the students that they will be playing the role of foraging honey bees. Divide the class into teams of three or four students. Each team chooses a hive. You may want to have students sit down in their hives as you explain the game.

Explain to the students that bees need pollen to feed to their young—pollen is high in the proteins needed for growth. In this game, you are going to focus on pollen collection. The object of the game is to collect as much pollen as possible in order to grow the hive. For every pollen token collected, their hive will be able to produce one more bee.

Bees can collect pollen from any of the food sources they want. They may only collect one pollen token at a time—they must then return to the hive to drop off the token before going back to collect another token.

Tell the students they will have a limited time to collect pollen. When the time is up, they must stop immediately and return to the hive.

Allow students enough time to collect 15-20 tokens per hive. This may only take a minute, depending on the children and the size of the playing area.

When time is up, ask students to count how many tokens they collected per hive. They will be tempted to declare a winner—the hive with the most tokens.

But...

Reveal to the students that some of the pollen in the environment was contaminated with pesticides. If a hive has one or more red tokens, they must divide their score in half, because even small amounts of pesticide slow down foraging bees so they can't collect as much pollen.

If a hive has collected more than 5 red tokens, they have collected so much pesticide that their entire colony dies.

After these adjustments are taken into account, you are welcome to declare a winner.

While students are still sitting in their hives, have them indicate by a show of hands which hives lost half their production and which hives died.

Most likely, you will notice a pattern to colony death. Colonies closest to the orchard and bean field will probably all be dead, while ones near the forest and meadow will probably have survived. Discuss why this might happen (orchards and crops are sprayed more frequently with pesticides). Discuss how our management of honey bees puts hives in exactly these dangerous locations, so they can pollinate the crops and fruit trees.

Conclusion

Lead students in a discussion of how we could manage honeybees to limit their exposure to pesticides while still pollinating crops.

Extension

Have students research the dangers facing honey bees, and develop "Save the Bees" posters that include ways in which we can help honey bees.

Game Set-up

Set up the playing area, as in the diagram below, on either pavement or grass. If pavement, draw hives, forest, meadow, orchard, and bean field with chalk. Label each hive with a number, and label each foraging area. If setting up on grass, use cones or hula hoops to represent hives and cardboard signs to represent foraging areas. Tokens can either be scattered around the area or placed in an ice cream container or small box. Plan on about 100 tokens per foraging area. Tokens should be of many different colours, so students don't suspect the colour is meaningful. In the Forest and Meadow areas, 10% of tokens should be red. In the Bean field and Orchard areas, 70% of tokens should be red. These ratios reflect the fact that pesticides are more frequently used in some areas than in others.

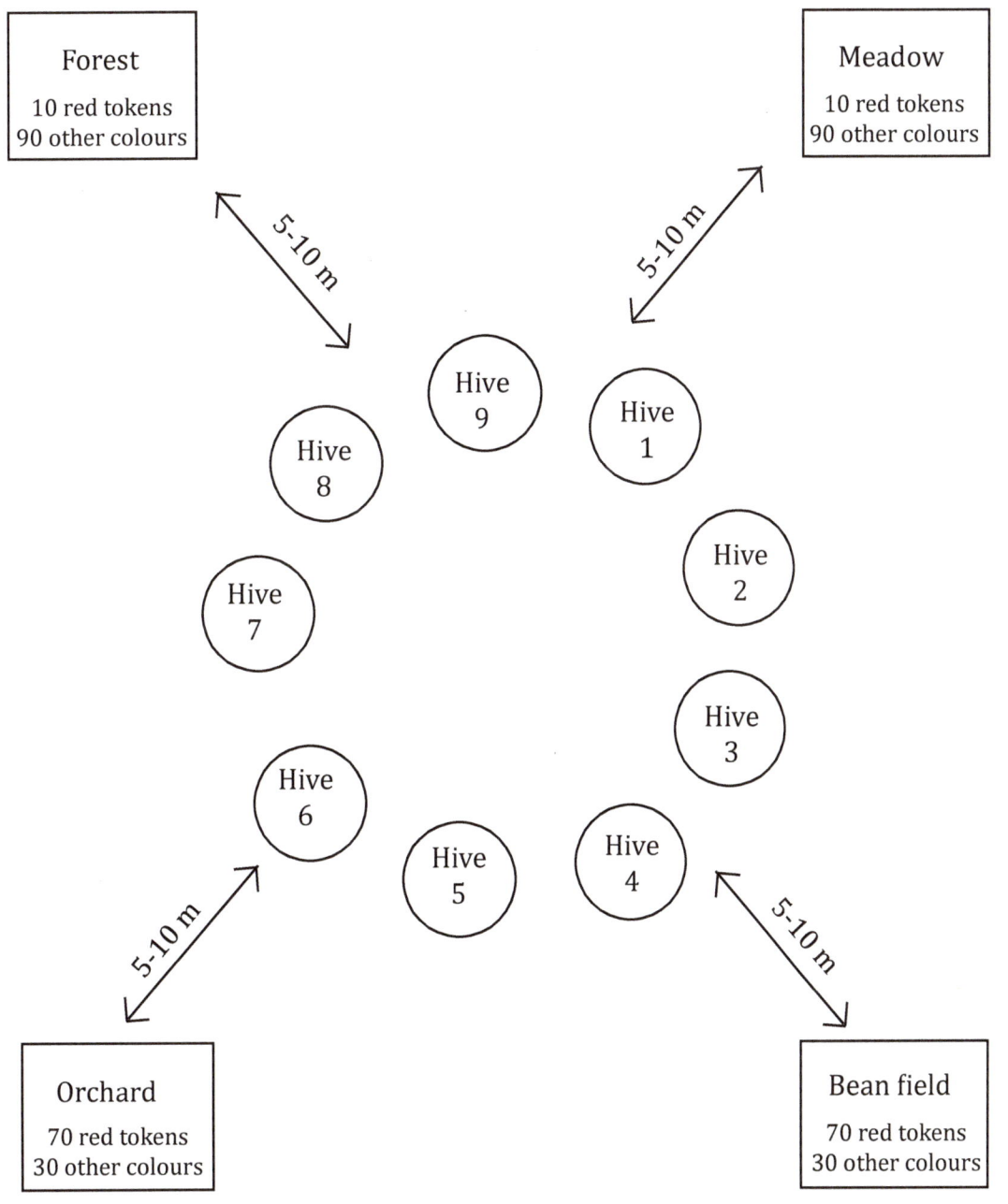

Insects In the Classroom

Measuring Diversity

A diversity index can be used to compare biodiversity in two places.

Summary

Students sample and compare biodiversity in two locations.

Learning Objectives

Students will:
1) Explain why scientists sample organisms.
2) Perform at least one type of sampling.
3) Calculate and compare diversity at different locations.

Curriculum Connections

Science, Living World, Ecology
Science, Nature of Science,
  Understanding about Science
  Investigating in Science
  Participating and Contributing

Vocabulary

sample, diversity index, biodiversity

Materials

Copies of Diversity Sampling Record Sheet (1 per group)
Pencils (1 per group)
Insect jars
For quadrant sampling: string circles (1 per group)
For sweep netting: nets (1 per group)
For pitfall traps: cups and boards (3 per group), trowels (1 per group)

Time: 1.5 - 2 hours or more if off site

Age: Years 4-6

Group size: Any

Introduction/Set-up

Understanding biodiversity can help us understand how an ecosystem functions, and how healthy an ecosystem is. Measuring biodiversity allows scientists to compare similar ecosystems in different locations, or to evaluate changes in one location over time.

Biodiversity is complex, and higher biodiversity does not necessarily mean a healthier ecosystem. For example, New Zealand's overall biodiversity has increased dramatically in the last 200 years because of the large number of introduced plants and animals. Few would argue, however, that New Zealand ecosystems are healthier because of these introductions. On the contrary, the introduced plants and animals have contributed to the decline of many of our native species. Because so many of our native species are found nowhere else, this represents an important ecological loss.

It is also important to understand that some ecosystems are naturally more diverse than others, but that ecosystems with low diversity are not necessarily unhealthy. Extreme environments like deserts, polar regions, and hot pools generally have low diversity, and cannot realistically be compared to ecosystems with naturally high diversity like tropical rainforests.

Measuring diversity

When scientists measure biodiversity, they cannot catalogue every single organism, even in a very small area. Instead they take a sample—they collect a subset of the organisms in their study area, and infer or predict total diversity from their sample. There are many different ways of doing this, and the method a scientist chooses depends upon exactly what she wants to know, as each method gives different information. By sampling diversity in exactly the same way in different locations, a scientist can compare the diversity of those locations.

Find two locations suitable for students to sample. The school grounds and a local park are good options.

38   Insects In the Classroom

Activity

Students will sample and identify insects to answer the question:

How does the insect diversity of your school grounds compare with the diversity of the local park?

Students don't have to be able to identify every living thing to work out the diversity of the school grounds or the local park. They do, however, need to be able to observe closely and identify whether organisms are the same as or different from one another. When recording organisms, if they don't know what something is, have them record its description instead. For example, an unknown insect might be "grey moth, 4mm long."

Sampling methods

Scientists sample insects in a variety of ways, depending on what type of insects they want to capture. Here are four simple ways your students can sample insects on your school grounds. Choose a method that suits your needs and resources.

Sweep netting

This technique is good for sampling flying and hopping insects in grassy areas.

Insect sweep nets are used just like you use a broom—they "sweep" the grass, knocking insects into the bag of the net. To sample using sweep nets, walk slowly along, sweeping back and forth with the net as you go. Make sure the net is brushing the grass (but not hitting the ground so hard as to damage the net or pick up dirt), and that you are turning the net between sweeps so that the insects are falling into the bag. Count each sweep as you make it. Make 10 sweeps and then quickly lift the net and hold it shut with one hand. Carefully collect all the insects from the net into jars and record what you have found. Do this at least three times in three locations. Be sure to release the insects when you have finished recording them.

Quadrant method

This method works well on lawns or meadows.

Spread out a string circle or a hula hoop on the ground to define your study area. Starting at one side of the circle, record all the insects you find within the circle, in the order you encounter them. Do this at least three times in different locations.

Pitfall traps

Pitfall traps sample insects and other arthropods that crawl along the ground.

Dig a hole and place a cup into the hole so that the rim is flush with the soil surface and the soil is packed around the outside of the cup. Place four small rocks around the cup and set a board on top of them. This will protect the trap from rain and debris, and create a sheltered place attractive to arthropods. Leave your trap in place for at least a week, collecting and recording the insects in it daily. Place at least three pitfall traps and record the catch in each one separately. Be sure to release the insects when you have finished recording them.

Observation

Timed observation is a good way to sample insects attracted to flowers.

Choose a spot with a lot of insect activity—a clump of flowers is a great location. Take some time to observe and identify the common visitors and to determine how you will record them. For example, you might see large green flies, large blue flies, small shiny flies, honey bees, small bumble bees, large bumble bees—make sure you can quickly distinguish and record the common visitors. You might come up with some short abbreviations for the insects you see, so you can record them quickly. Once you are confident you can record visitors quickly, start your actual sampling. Record every visitor to your flowers for a set amount of time, or until you reach 10 individuals. Do this at least three times in different locations.

Calculating diversity

Regardless of what you've sampled or how you've sampled it, you can calculate a diversity index for your sample. A diversity index is a measure that takes into account both the total number of organisms and also the relative numbers of each organism. The Sequential Sampling Index yields a number between 0 and 1 that can be used to compare the diversity of different locations

(Remembering, of course, that you can only compare samples taken exactly the same way). The higher the Diversity Index (the closer to 1), the more diverse the community.

Regardless of how you sampled, you should end up with a list of organisms for each sample. It is important, when you are recording your samples, that you record organisms in the order in which you encountered them—i.e. you want a random list—don't group all the same type on your list. If you mistakenly did this, you can easily fix it by writing the name of each individual organism on a slip of paper, putting them into a hat, and drawing them out, re-recording them in the order you draw them out.

Once you have your random list, determine the number of "runs" in each trial. A run is a series of the same organism (a new run starts whenever you come to a different organism). In the sample list below, each run is circled.

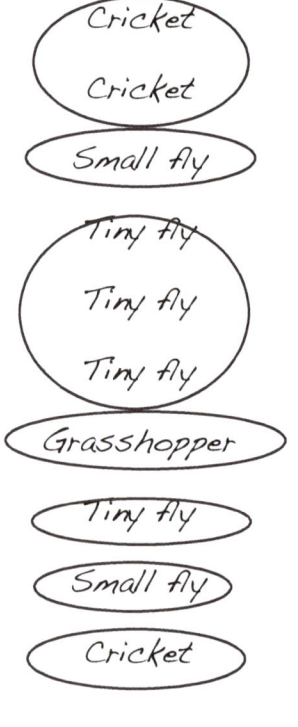

Counting the number of circles, we have 7 runs in this sample. To calculate the Diversity Index for the sample, divide the number of runs by the number of organisms in the sample. For the example above:

Diversity Index = # runs / # individuals

Diversity Index = 7 / 10 = 0.7

Find the diversity index of each of the three samples you collected, then find the average diversity score for that location.

Extension/discussion

1. Which location had a higher average diversity score? Why do you think this was the case?

2. What factors might affect insect diversity on your school grounds?

3. How might you increase biodiversity on the school grounds?

4. Why do you need to take three separate samples and find an average Diversity Index?

5. Do you think insect diversity would increase if you increased plant diversity? Does it matter what type of plants you plant? How could you find out the answers to these questions?

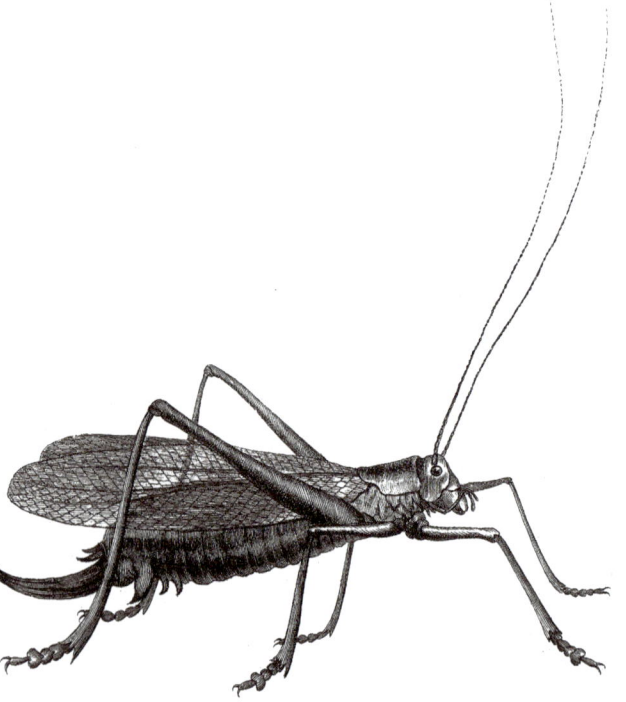

Diversity Sampling Record Sheet

Sampling Method: _____

	First Trial	Second Trial	Third Trial
1			
2			
3			
4			
5			
6			
7			
8			
9			
10			
Number of Runs			
Diversity score (# runs ÷10)			

Average Diversity Score:

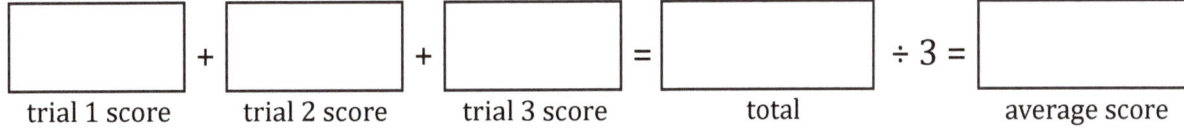

trial 1 score + trial 2 score + trial 3 score = total ÷ 3 = average score

Insects In the Classroom   41

Cricket Olympics

Many insects have amazing physical abilities.

Summary

Students test how far crickets can jump and compare it to their own jumping ability.

Learning Objectives

Students will:
1) Describe how cricket and human abilities differ.
2) Describe how cricket jumping works.

Curriculum Connections

Science, Living World, Life Processes

Vocabulary

adaptation

Materials

Live crickets in small containers
Chalk
Calculators
Rulers
Tape measures

Time: 45 minutes

Age: Years 3-6

Group size: Any

Introduction/Set-up

Because of their size and the structure of their bodies, insects are often proportionally stronger and faster than people. The reason for this is partly explained by simple geometry.

Insects seem incredibly strong because their muscles (whose strength is proportional to their cross-sectional area) are moving a very small mass compared to the muscles' cross-sectional area. But if we increase the size of an insect to that of a human, the ratio of body mass to muscle cross-section rises dramatically. Why?

As an animal increases in size, the muscle cross-sectional surface area increases in proportion to the square of the length of the animal (because surface area is measured in two dimensions), but the animal's volume (and hence, mass) increases in proportion to the cube of the length (because volume is measured in three dimensions). So as an arthropod's size increases, its volume to surface ratio goes up. An insect the size of a human wouldn't seem nearly as strong as a real insect.

In addition to the advantage of their small size, insects have other adaptations which increase their physical abilities. Crickets and grasshoppers use an interesting method of powering their jumps that increases the speed and distance they can jump.

When we jump, our leg muscles directly apply the force to our legs to make them straighten and hurl us into the air.

Grasshoppers and crickets don't use their muscles directly to jump. Instead, they use their leg muscles to compress a rubber-like substance called resilin in their knee joints, and to warp their exoskeleton. This stores energy in the leg. When they want to jump they release the energy, and the resilin and exoskeleton spring back into shape, causing the legs to straighten and the insect to fly into the air. The action is very much like that of a bouncy ball, which compresses upon impact with the ground, then springs back into shape and into the air.

Explain to the students that they are going to test the jumping ability of crickets and compare it to their own jumping ability.

42 Insects In the Classroom

Activity

Testing the crickets

Cricket testing can be done as a whole class or in small groups, depending on how many crickets you have available.

Place individual crickets into small containers (the smaller the better). With a ruler, measure and record the cricket's body length (not including antennae or cerci and ovipositor). This can be difficult—putting crickets in the refrigerator for 15 minutes can slow them down somewhat for measuring. Make sure they warm up before testing their jumps.

Mark a starting spot on the floor or playground with chalk. Invert the cricket container on top of the mark. When the students are ready, lift the container off the cricket. The cricket should jump, but if it is reluctant to do so, give it a small nudge. Watch carefully, and place another chalk mark where the cricket lands. Measure the distance travelled. Record at least three jumps and circle the longest one.

Testing the students

Using the tape measure, have students measure and record their height.

Draw a line on the floor or playground with chalk. Have students do the standing long jump from this line, and measure the distance jumped. Record at least three jumps and circle the longest one.

Conclusion

It is unfair to compare the actual distances the crickets and the students jumped, given the enormous size differences between them. Instead, have the students calculate the number of body lengths each jumped. Use the longest jumps recorded for each individual.

Body lengths jumped = Distance jumped ÷ Body length (or height)

For example, if a 1 cm long cricket jumped 35 cm, it would have jumped 35 body lengths (35 ÷ 1). If a 125 cm tall student jumped 100 cm, she would have jumped 0.8 body lengths (100 cm ÷ 125 cm).

Calculate how far students could jump if they had the abilities of crickets.

Using the cricket's longest jump, in body lengths, calculate how far each student could jump if they could jump as many of their own body lengths.

Jumping distance = # body lengths jumped by a cricket x height of the student

For example: if our 125 cm tall student could jump 35 body lengths, she could jump 4375 cm (125 x 35), or 43.75 metres! Measure this distance on the playground so students can see how far it is.

Explain to the students how crickets are able to jump so far, and why people aren't able to do so.

Extension

1. Have students research some of the other amazing abilities of insects.

2. Have students write a story about a person with the jumping ability of a cricket.

Colouring Sheets

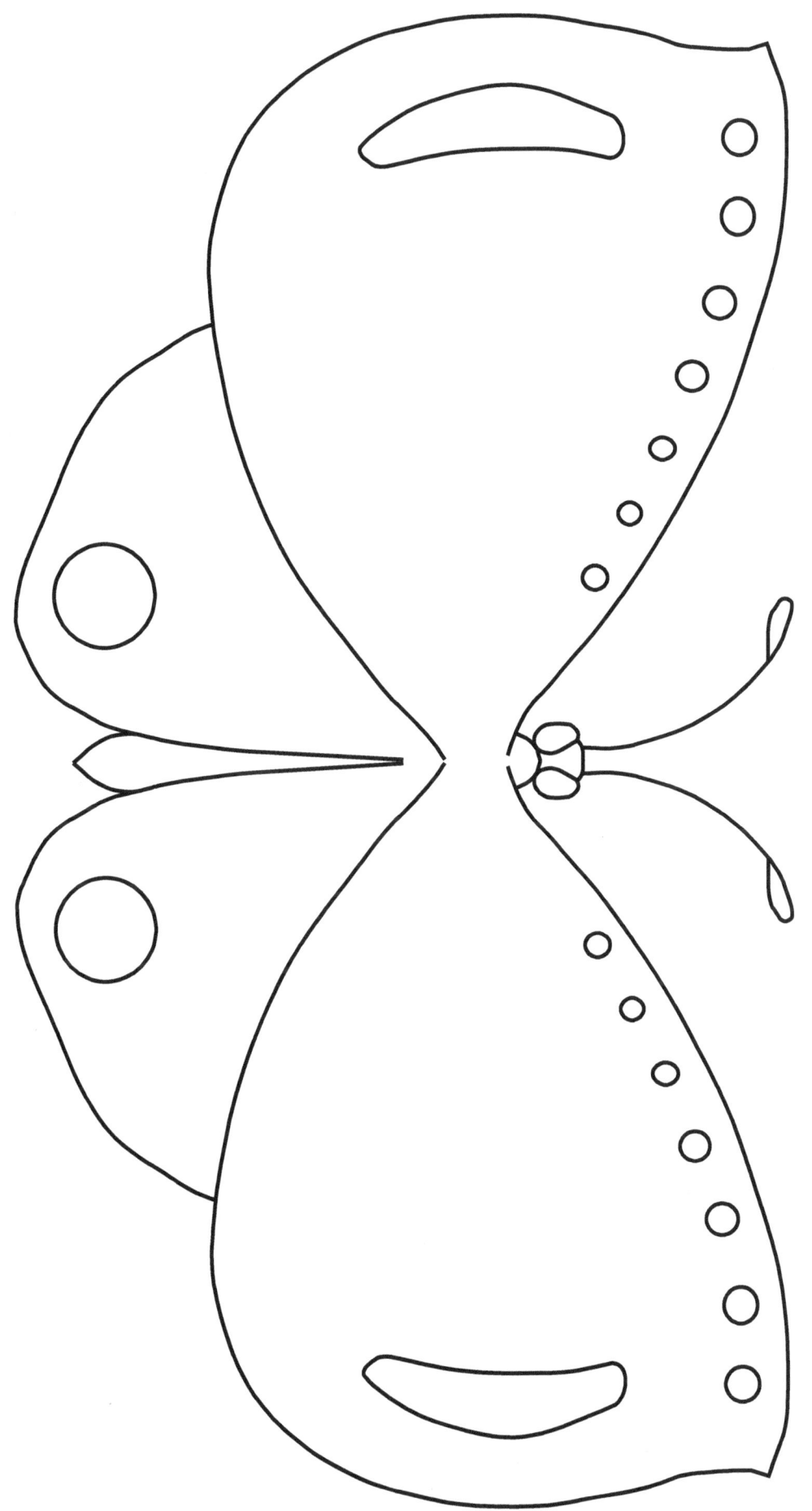

Butterfly

Insects In the Classroom 45

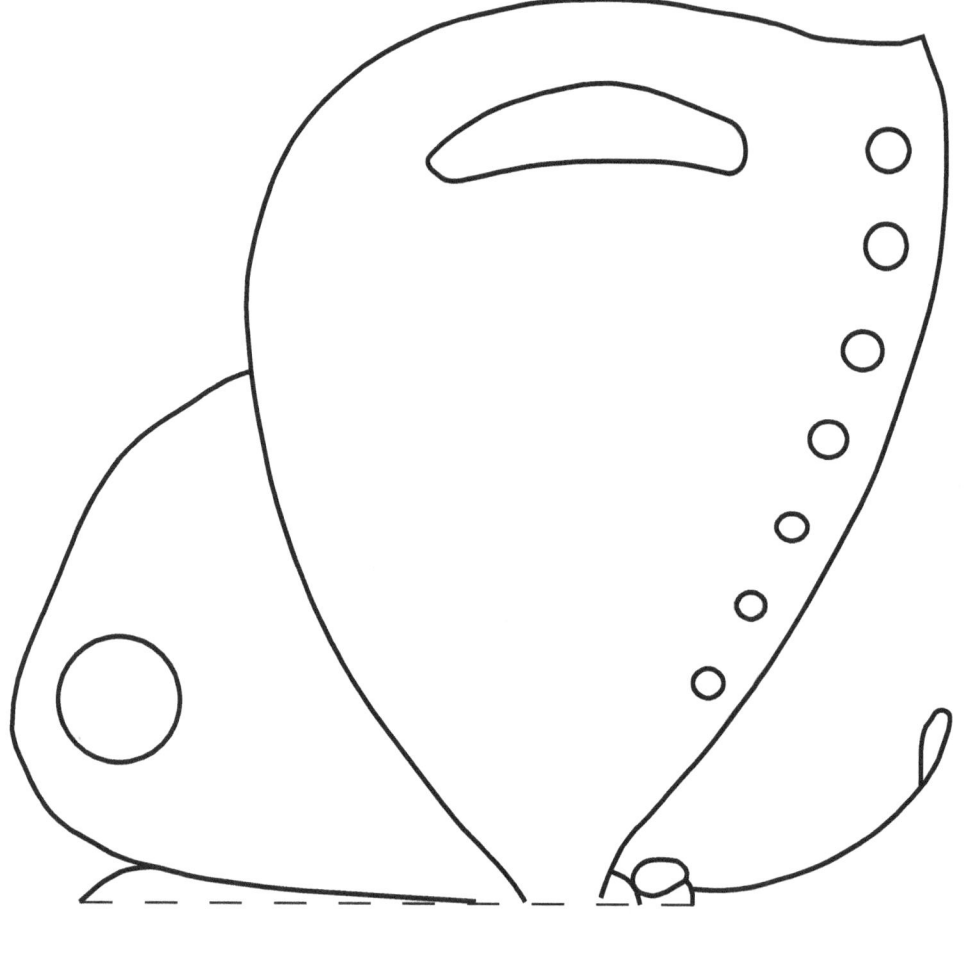

Butterfly

Draw the other half and colour it in.

46 Insects In the Classroom

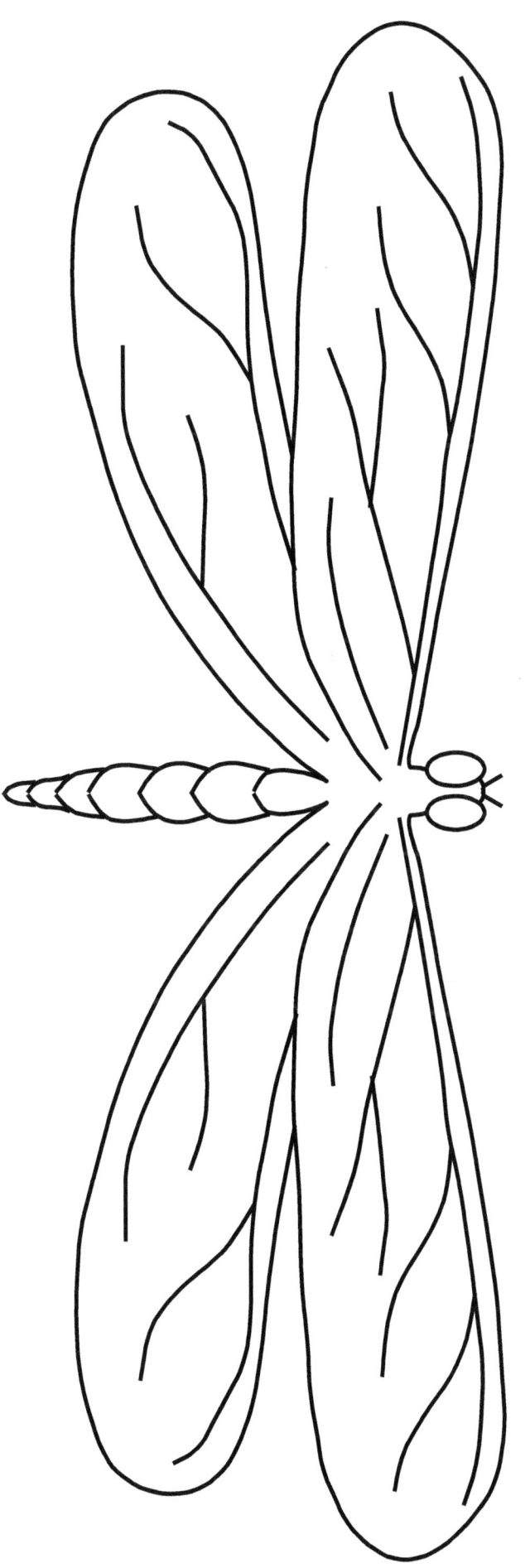

Dragonfly

Insects In the Classroom 47

Dragonfly

Draw the other half and colour it in.

48 Insects In the Classroom

Huhu beetle

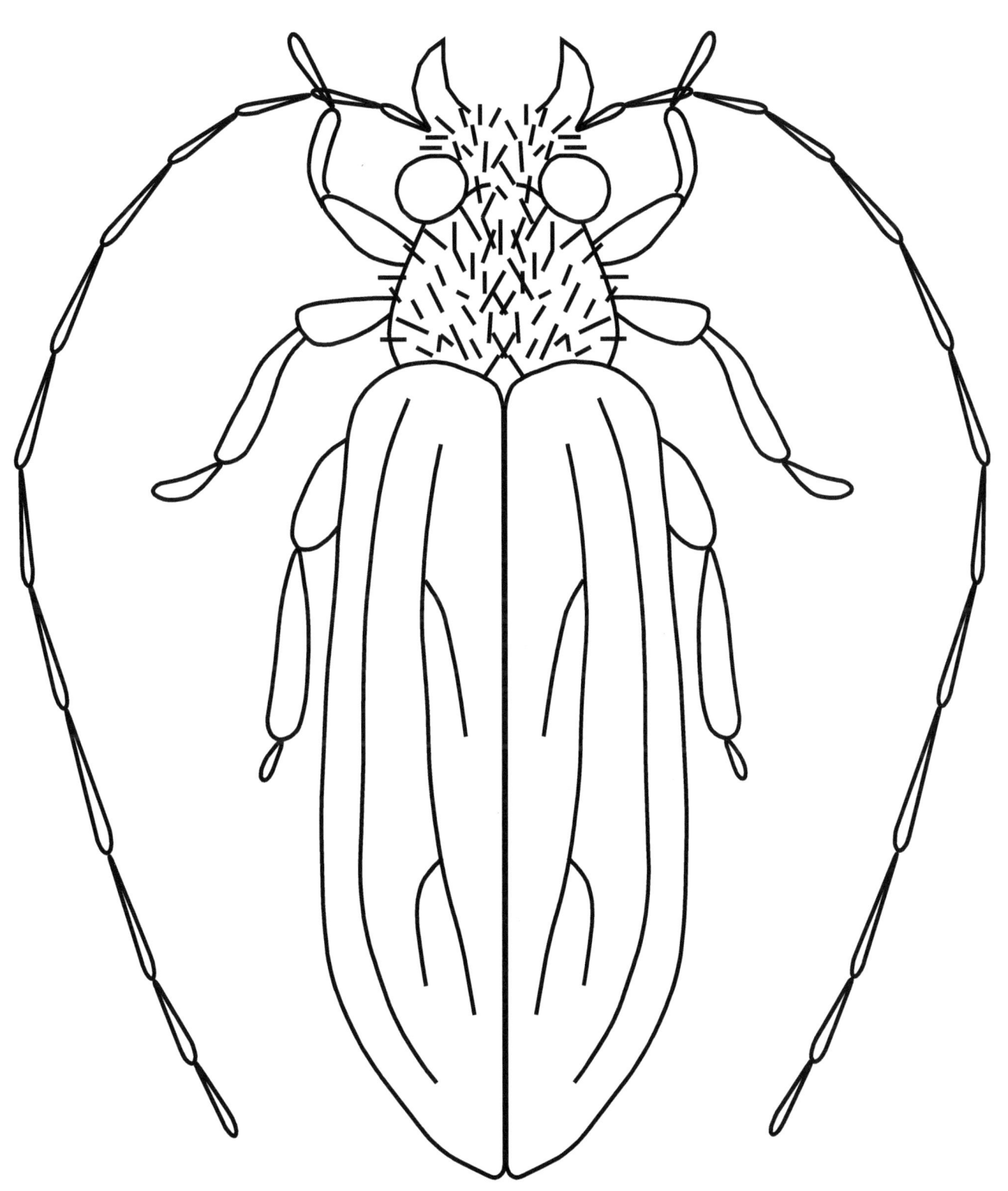

Huhu beetle

Draw the other half and colour it in.

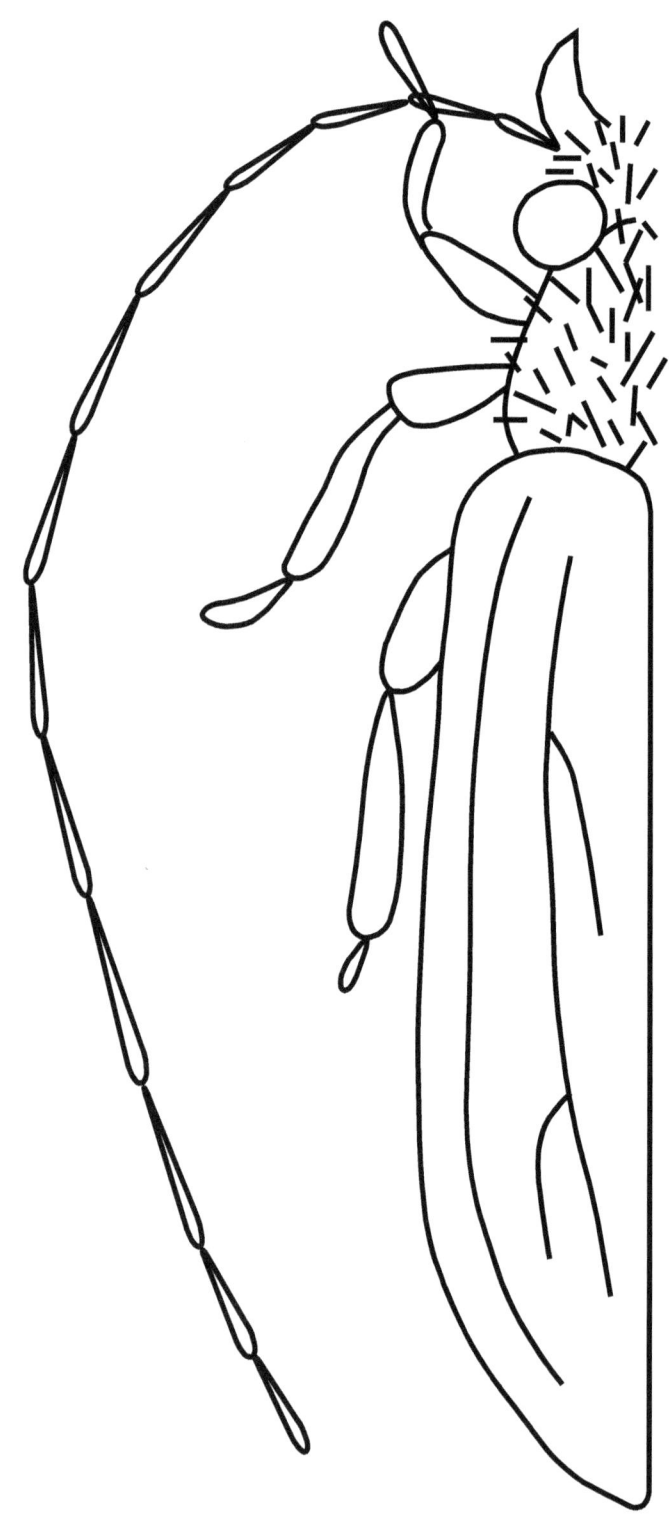

Ladybug

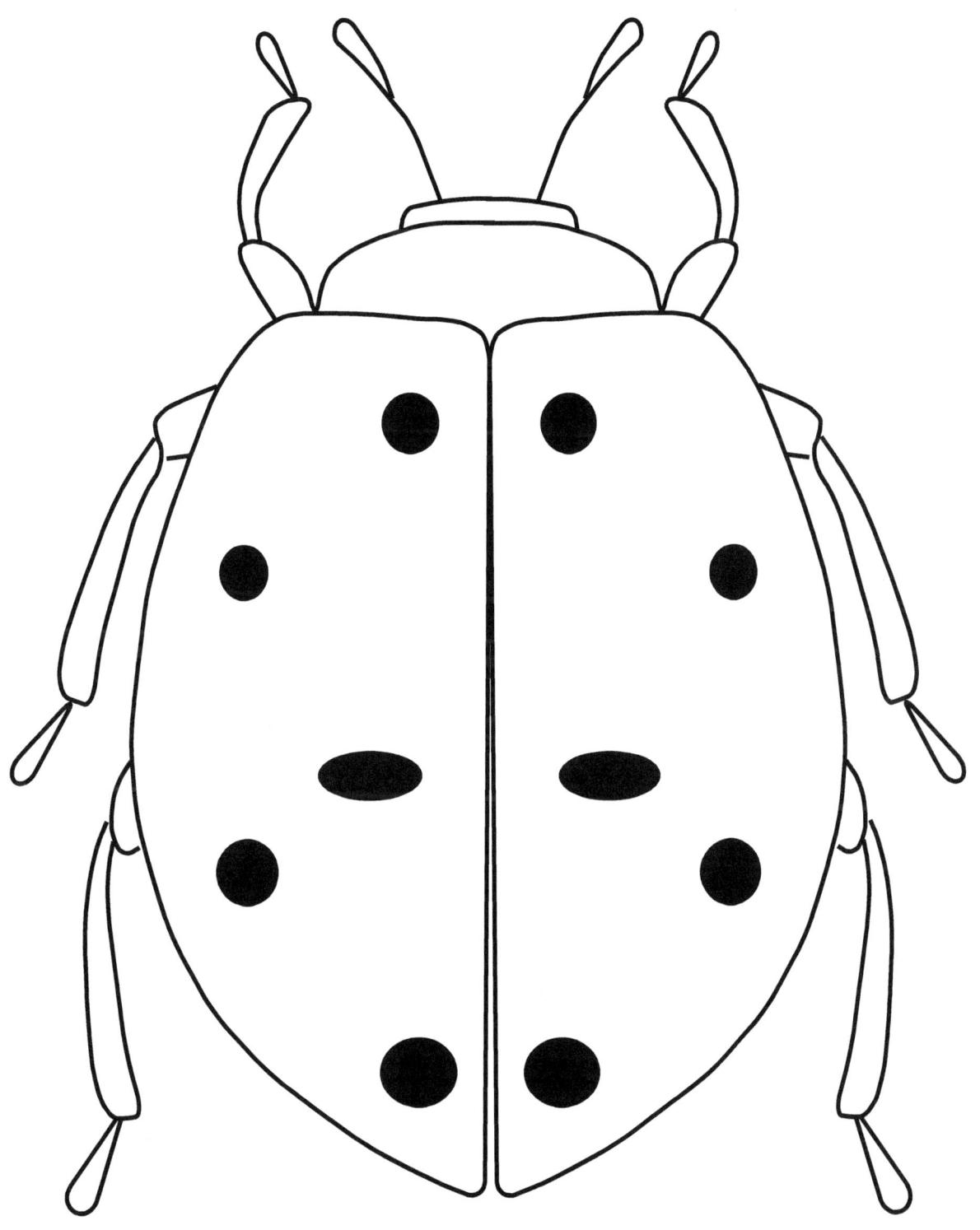

Insects In the Classroom 51

Ladybug

Draw the other half and colour it in.

52 Insects In the Classroom

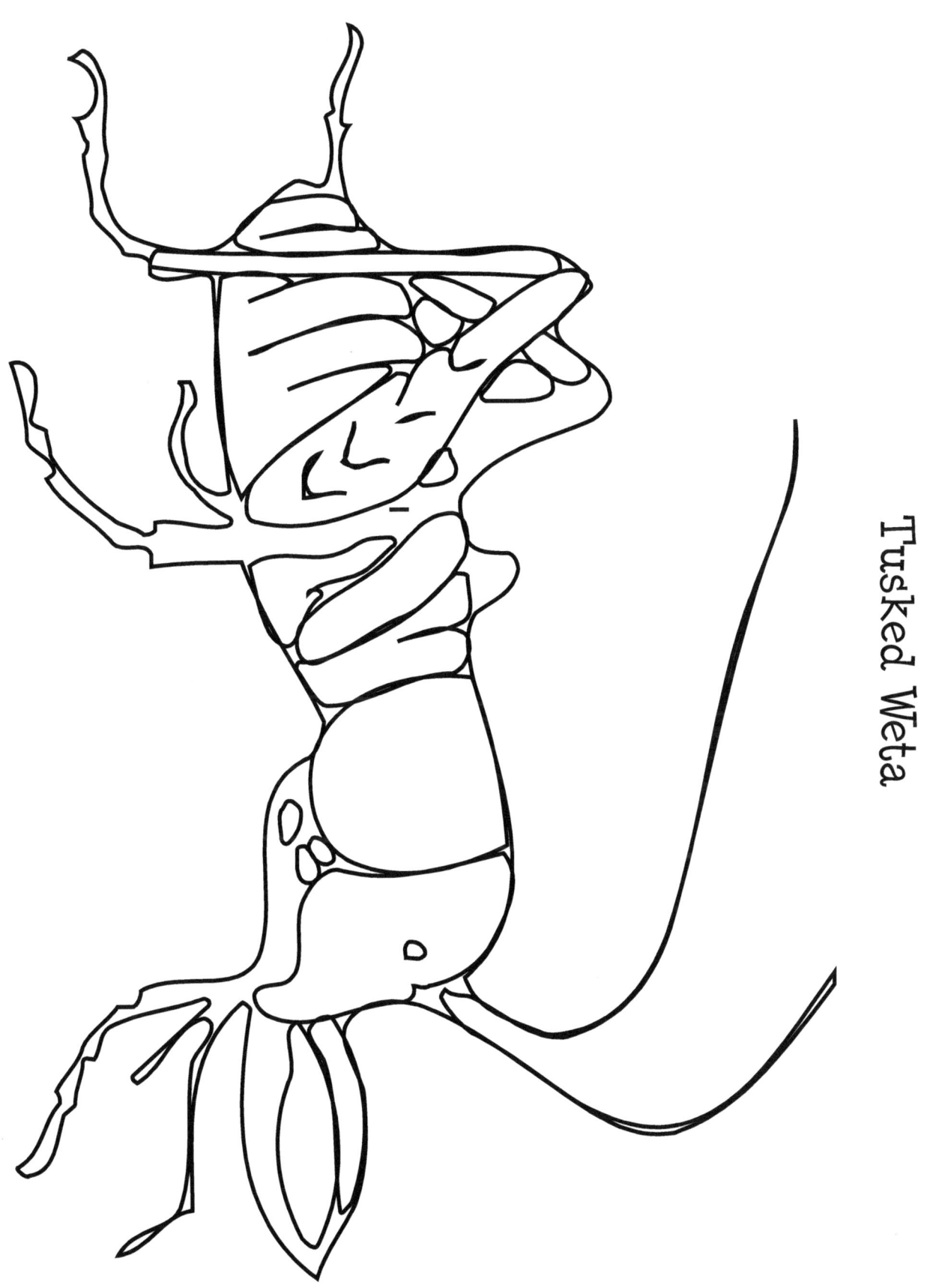

Tusked Weta

Worksheets / Puzzles

Bug Basics Word Search

Circle the buggy words in the wordfind below.

```
X A R O H T I S S E N Y J G S
W N G O P G A R G O J D F W E
T T J N C R W O T N T X U C Y
J E R A Y Q M E T Q I B X Q E
S N D D U Y L L H K F W Q G D
C N J S D E S A R F K T I I N
B A G P K K B N H D Y P M B U
U E M S A D A P T A T I O N O
L U O O O Z N W O E Y E O O P
W X T M U Y J S V H E L P G M
E Y E J G F G L N F J I Q V O
A N D X X Z L V K D N P F N C
D Z R V M D Y A Z K N P W L P
Z Z K A B C H W G I G K G D V
T G H E R V Q E V E G F H D P
```

ABDOMEN
ADAPTATION
ANTENNAE
CAMOUFLAGE
COMPOUND EYES
EXOSKELETON
HEAD
LEGS
THORAX
WINGS

Insects In the Classroom 55

Bug Basics

Fill in the blanks below to review what you know about insects.

Insects all have____legs, 3 body parts, and_____antennae. The body parts are called the_____, _____, and _____.

Insects use their antennae for_____.

The hard shell on the outside of an insect is called an _____.

An _____ is something that helps an insect survive.

My favourite insect is a _____. One of its adaptations is _____.

Draw your favourite insect below. Label the parts.

Buggy Crossword

ACROSS

2 Land-dwelling crustacean
6 Has six legs
7 An animal with no backbone
8 Has a long, segmented body and no visible head
9 Its name means hundred-footed
10 Insects are the only invertebrates with them
12 Jointed-legs
13 Insects have two, spiders have none, slaters have four
14 You'll find this slimy pest in your lettuces

DOWN

1 Its name means thousand-footed
3 The hard outer shell of arthropods
4 Sometimes called daddy long-legs
5 Spins silk
11 Carries its shelter on its back

Adaptation Worksheet

Draw a line to match each animal with its adaptation.

Ladybug   Large front legs for catching prey

Grasshopper   Loud songs for attracting mates

Spider   Bright colours to warn predators it's poisonous

Praying Mantis   Piercing-sucking mouthparts for drinking sap and blood

Stick Insect   Camouflage for avoiding predators

Honey Bee   Silk for capturing prey

Cicada   Sting for defending itself

Mosquito   Jumping legs to escape predators

Imagine an insect adapted to life in your classroom. Draw your imaginary insect below.
What adaptations does it have?

Identifying Insects

Picture Key to Garden and Park Invertebrates

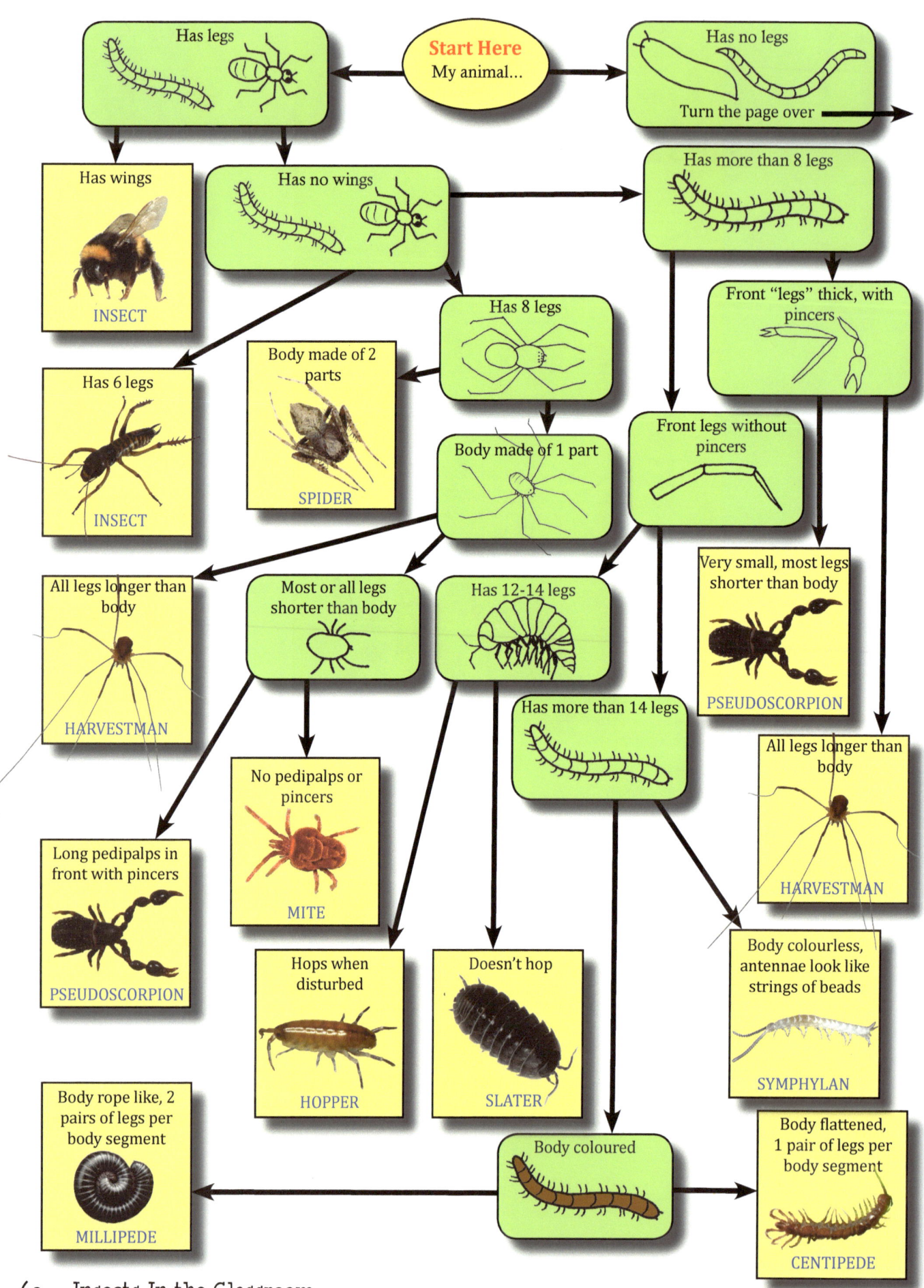

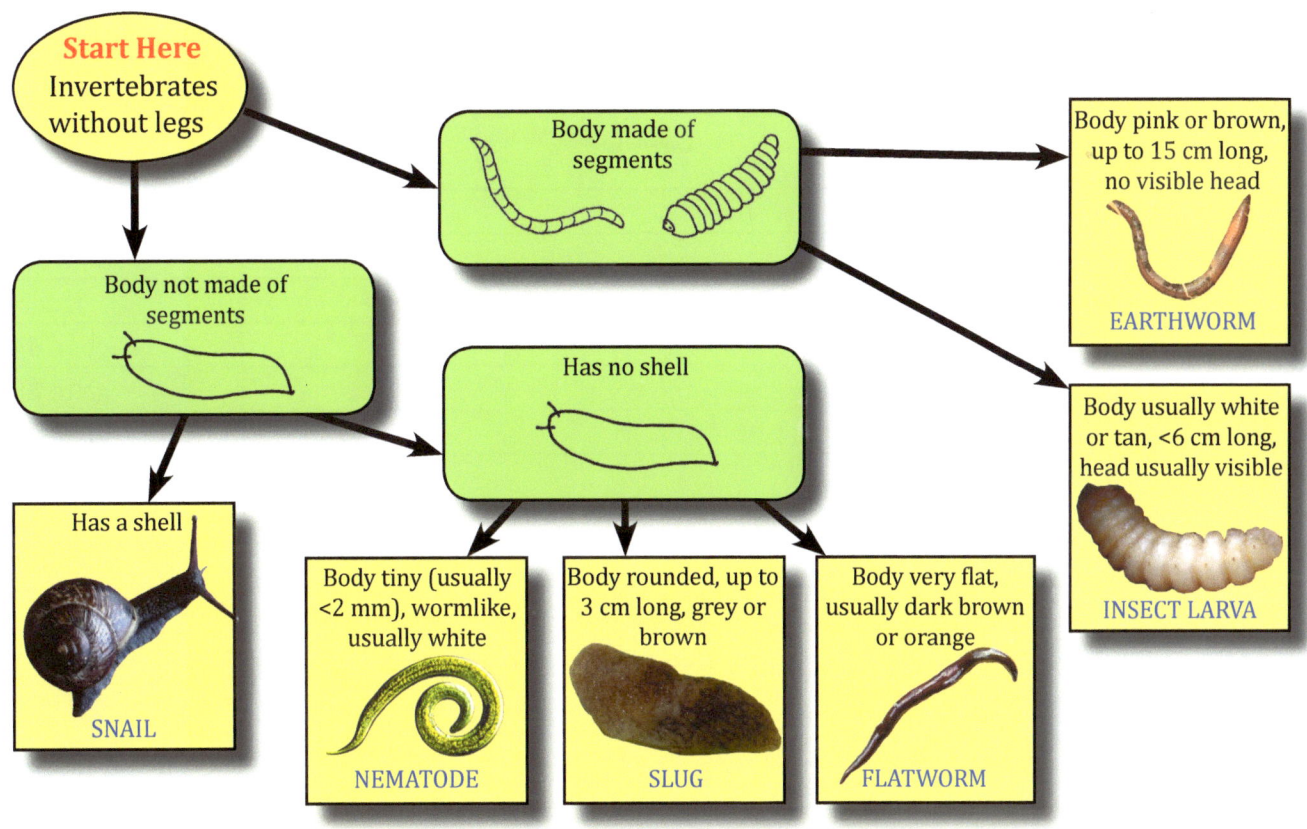

More About These Invertebrates

INSECTS have 6 legs, 2 antennae, and 3 main body parts. Most adult insects have wings. They are the only invertebrates with wings.

INSECT LARVAE come in many shapes, sizes, and colours. Some have legs, some don't. Insect larvae never have wings; only adults do.

SPIDERS have 8 legs, no antennae, and 2 main body parts. Spiders spin silk, and use poison fangs to paralyse their prey.

SNAILS and SLUGS have no legs. They move with a muscular "foot" that glides over a trail of slime. A snail's shell grows with it.

HARVESTMEN have 8 legs, no antennae, and 1 main body part. They do not spin silk, and do not have poison fangs.

NEMATODES are usually colourless and less than 2 mm long. There are millions of them in every shovelful of soil.

EARTHWORMS have no legs, and a long body made of segments. Most are less than 15 cm long, but some can reach 1.5 metres.

CENTIPEDES and MILLIPEDES may look similar, but they live very different lives. Millipedes are scavengers, eating mostly dead plants. Centipedes are predators that kill other invertebrates with poison fangs.

Photos: Snail--Hakan Svensson; Symphylan--Sonia Martinez; Insect Larva--Charlotte Simmonds; Mite--Olaf Leillinger; Millipede--Eiten F; Nematode--CSIRO; Hopper--US National Park Service, Oregon Caves National Park; Flatworm and Pseudoscorpion--public domain; all other photos--Robinne Weiss

Insects In the Classroom

Key to Garden and Park Invertebrates

1	a	has legs	go to #2
	b	has no legs	go to #3
2	a	has wings	Insect
	b	has no wings	go to #4
3	a	body made of segments	go to #8
	b	body not made of segments (may have a shell)	go to #9
4	a	has 6 legs	Insect
	b	has 8 legs	go to #5
	c	has more than 8 legs	go to #10
5	a	body made of two distinct parts	Spider
	b	body made of one part	go to #6
6	a	body tiny (<5 mm), legs short	go to #16
	b	body up to 10 mm long, legs longer than body	Harvestman
7	a	body small (about 1 mm) and legs short	Mite
	b	body up to 10 mm long, legs longer than body	Harvestman
8	a	body may be up to 1.5 m long (though usually much smaller), usually pinkish brown, no visible head	Earthworm
	b	body variable in size and colour, head usually visible	Insect larva
9	a	has a shell	Snail
	b	has no shell	go to #11
10	a	front "legs" thick, with pincers at the end	go to #17
	b	front legs without pincers	go to #12
11	a	body tiny (usually less than 2 mm), wormlike, usually whitish	Nematode
	b	body rounded, up to 3 cm long, grey or brown	Slug
	c	body very flat, usually dark brown or orange	Flatworm
12	a	12-14 legs	go to #13
	b	more than 14 legs	go to #14
13	a	doesn't jump	Slater
	b	hops when disturbed	Hopper
14	a	body completely colourless, antennae look like strings of beads	Symphylan
	b	body coloured	go to #15
15	a	body rope-like, legs attached to underside of body, 2 pairs of legs per body segment	Millipede
	b	body flattened, legs attached to side, 1 pair of legs per body segment	Centipede
16	a	long pedipalps in front with pincers	Pseudoscorpion
	b	no long pedipalps with pincers	Mite
17	a	body tiny (<5 mm), legs mostly shorter than body	Pseudoscorpion
	b	body up to 10 mm long, legs mostly longer than body	Harvestman

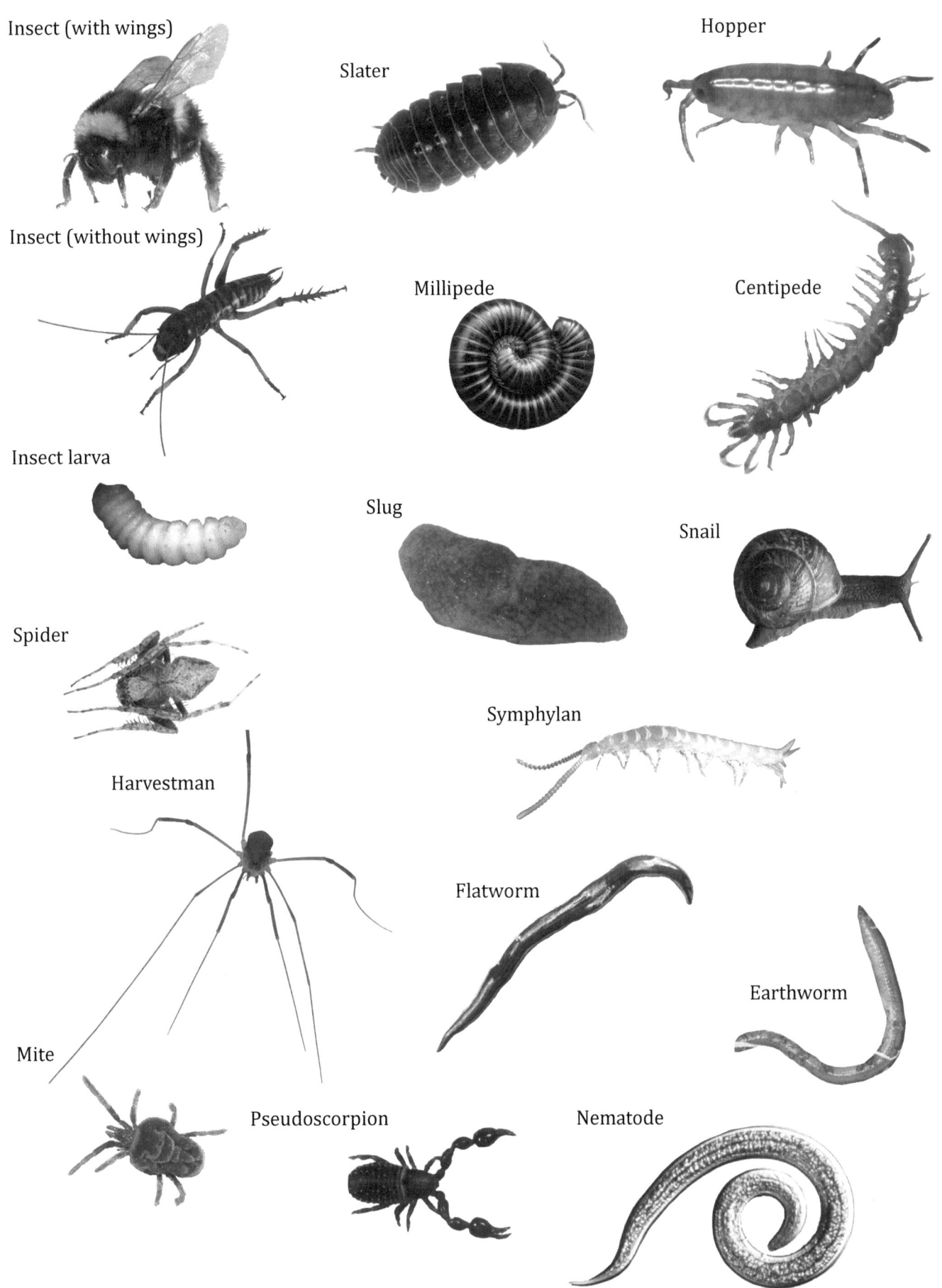

Key to Common Garden and Park Insects in New Zealand

(adult insects only)

1	a	has wings	go to #2
	b	has no wings	go to #3
2	a	has 1 pair of wings	Diptera (flies)
	b	has 2 pairs wings	go to #4
3	a	jumps	Orthoptera (grasshoppers, crickets, weta)
	b	doesn't jump	go to #6
4	a	front wings form a hard shell	Coleoptera (beetles)
	b	front wings don't form a shell	go to #9
5	a	pincers at the end of the abdomen	Dermaptera (earwigs; actually have wings, but not usually visible)
	b	no pincers at the end of the abdomen	go to #6
6	a	body long and stick-like	Phasmatodea (stick insects)
	b	body not shaped like a stick	go to #7
7	a	body rounded, often green or grey, found on plants	Hemiptera (aphids)
	b	body has a 'waist', dark coloured, often found on the ground	Hymenoptera (ants)
8	a	wings covered in scales	Lepidoptera (butterflies, moths)
	b	wings clear, membranous	go to #9

64   Insects In the Classroom

9	a	mouthparts straw-like (piercing-sucking)	Hemiptera (plant hoppers, cicadas, aphids, true bugs)
	b	mouthparts not straw-like	go to #10
10	a	large pincers at end of abdomen	Dermaptera (earwigs)
	b	no pincers at end of abdomen	go to #11
11	a	wings showy	go to #12
	b	wings not showy, held flat against back	go to #13
12	a	usually found near water, strong fliers	Odonata (dragonflies, damselflies)
	b	often found near flowers, may have warning colouration	Hymenoptera (bees, wasps, ants)
13	a	body flattened	Blattodea (cockroaches)
	b	body not flattened	go to #14
14	a	front legs enlarged for capturing prey (raptorial)	Mantodea (mantids)
	b	back legs enlarged for jumping (saltatorial)	Orthoptera (grasshoppers)

Resources

Books

NZ-specific:

A Mini Guide to the Identification of New Zealand Insects (Andrew Crowe; Penguin, 2010)
Stick Insects (NZ Wild) (Steve Trewick and Mary Morgan-Richards; Raupo Publishing, 2005)
The Life-Size Guide to Insects and Other Land Invertebrates of New Zealand (Andrew Crowe; Penguin Books, 1999)
All About New Zealand's Garden Wildlife (Dave Gunson; New Holland Publishers, 2012)
The Monarch Butterfly in New Zealand (George Gibbs; Entomological Society of New Zealand, 2013)
New Zealand Garden Wildlife to Read, Colour and Keep (Dave Gunson; New Holland Publishing, 2012)
An Illustrated Guide to Some New Zealand Insect Families (Elizabeth A. Grant; Manaaki Whenua Press, 1999)
Butterflies and Moths of New Zealand (Brian Parkinson and Brian Patrick; Reed Books, 2000)
Managing Pests and Diseases: a Handbook for New Zealand Gardeners (Rob Lucas; Craig Potton Publishing, 2005)
Which New Zealand Insect? (Andrew Crowe; Penguin Books, 2002)
Which New Zealand Spider? (Andrew Crowe; Penguin Books, 2007)
Spiders of New Zealand and their Worldwide Kin (Ray Forster and Lyn Forster; University of Otago Press, 1999)
New Zealand Weta (George Gibbs; Reed Books, 1998)
The Weta Book: A guide to the identification of wetas (Mike Meads; Manaaki Whenua Press, 1990)
Keeping Wetas in Captivity (Paul Barrett, ed. G.W. Ramsay; Wellington Zoological Gardens, 1991)
Life-Size Guide to New Zealand Native Ferns: featuring the unique caterpillars which feed on them (Andrew Crowe; Penguin Books, 2004)
A Photographic Guide to Insects of New Zealand (Brian Parkinson and Don Horne; New Holland Publishers, 2007)
Biological Control Agents for Weeds in New Zealand: a field guide (Lynley Hayes; Landcare Research New Zealand, Ltd, 2005; available as a free pdf at: https://www.landcareresearch.co.nz/__data/assets/pdf_file/0019/43138/weeds_field_guide.pdf)

General Entomology:

The Practical Entomologist: an Introductory Guide to Observing and Understanding the World of Insects (Rick Imes; Simon and Schuster Inc, 1992)
The Insects: an Outline of Entomology, 4th Edition (P.J. Gullan and P.S. Cranston; John Wiley & Sons Ltd, 2010)
Bugs in the System: Insects and Their Impact on Human Affairs (May R. Berenbaum; Addison-Wesley Publishing Company Inc., 1995)
Spineless Wonders: Strange Tales from the Invertebrate World (Richard Conniff; Henry Holt and Company, 1996)
Man Eating Bugs: The Art and Science of Eating Insects (Peter Menzel and Faith D'Aluiso; Material World, 1998)

Educational Resources

Science Resource Box--http://scienceresourcebox.co.nz/information/information&information_id=7
Bug Wise: Thirty Incredible Insect Investigations and Arachnid Activities (Pamela M. Hickman; Addison-Wesley Publishing Company Inc, 1990)
Insects and Spiders: Mind-boggling Experiments You Can Turn into Science Fair Projects (Janice VanCleave; John Wiley and Sons Inc, 1998)
Bug Camp: Where Every Day's an Adventure (Tim Forrest and Jen Hamel; Moon Dance Press, 2016)

Online Resources

NZ-based:

Landcare Research Insects and Spiders Resources--http://www.landcareresearch.co.nz/resources/teaching/Insects-and-spiders
Te Papa Spiders of New Zealand Teaching Resources--https://www.tepapa.govt.nz/learn/for-educators/teaching-resources/spiders-new-zealand-teaching-resource

Entomological Society of New Zealand--http://ento.org.nz/
Apiculture New Zealand--http://apinz.org.nz/

International:

The Pennsylvania State University Department of Entomology, Education and Outreach--http://ento.psu.edu/public
Iowa State Entomology Index of Internet Resources--http://www.ent.iastate.edu/list/directory/158/vid/5
Texas A&M University Agrilife Extension--http://www.texasinsects.org/

Entomological suppliers

BioQuip Products--http://www.bioquip.com/
Australian Entomological Supplies--http://www.entosupplies.com.au/
Biosuppliers (live insects)--http://biosuppliers.nz/
Zonda (live insects)--http://www.zonda.net.nz/
Insects Direct (live crickets)--http://www.insectdirect.co.nz/

Citizen Science

NatureWatch NZ, where students can record observations of nature, and engage with scientists--http://naturewatch.org.nz/

Insects In the Classroom

Glossary

Abdomen	The rearmost region of an insect or spider's body. Houses reproductive, respiratory, and digestive organs.
Adaptation	A feature of an organism that increases its ability to survive and reproduce.
Antenna (plural, antennae)	Sensory organs attached to the head of insects and some other arthropods. Used for smell, feel, taste, and hearing.
Aposematic colouration	Bright colours that warn predators an animal is poisonous.
Arthropod	A phylum of organisms with exoskeletons and jointed legs.
Ballooning	A type of locomotion in which a young spider spins a thread of silk and allows the wind to blow it away, carrying the spider with it.
Biodiversity	The diversity of life. All the living things in a particular place.
Camouflage	Hiding by looking like the background.
Cephalothorax	The front body region of a spider. Eyes, mouthparts, pedipalps, and legs are all attached here.
Cerci	Sensory appendages on the tip of an insect's abdomen.
Classification	The organisation of living things into groups, such as kingdom, phylum, class, order, family, genus, and species.
Colony Collapse Disorder	A syndrome in which honey bee colonies die quickly through the disappearance of worker bees. Thought to be caused by a range of factors that act together to weaken the hive.
Compound eye	A cluster of simple eyes (ommatidia).
Communication	Sharing information.
Diversity index	A measure of biodiversity.
Entomophagy	Eating insects.
Evolve	To change genetically over time.
Evolution	The act of changing genetically over time.
Exoskeleton	A skeleton on the outside of the body.
Finite	Of limited quantity.
Forage	To look for food.
Habitat	An area in which an organism lives.
Head	The front body region of an insect. Eyes, mouthparts, and antennae are attached here.
Hemolymph	Insect 'blood'. Carries nutrients, hormones, and immune defences, but usually not oxygen.
Hypothesis	An educated guess as to the outcome of an experiment.

Instar	A stage of insect growth between moults.
Larva (plural, larvae)	The immature phase of an insect that undergoes complete metamorphosis.
Mandibles	An insect's 'jaws'. In chewing-type mouthparts, mandibles are used for grasping and tearing apart food.
Metamorphosis	A change in body shape over an animal's lifetime.
Moulting	Shedding the exoskeleton.
Natural selection	The process whereby not all individuals survive to reproduce. Natural selection can lead to the evolution of adaptations.
Niche	The particular space and conditions in which an organism lives.
Nymph	The immature phase of an insect that undergoes incomplete metamorphosis.
Ocellus (plural, ocelli)	Simple eyes of insects. Most insects have three located in a triangle on the top of the head. Ocelli are involved in regulating the insect's diurnal schedule.
Ommatidium (plural, ommatidia)	A single unit of an insect's compound eye.
Ovipositor	Egg-laying tube, usually on the tip of the abdomen. Common in wasps, crickets, wētā, and grasshoppers.
Pedipalp	A sensory appendage of a spider, attached to the cephalothorax.
Pesticide	A chemical used to kill animal pests.
Phylogeny	The evolutionary history of an organism.
Pollination	The transfer of pollen from one flower to another for fertilisation.
Population	The number of individuals of a particular species.
Predator	An animal that eats other animals.
Prey	An animal that is eaten by other animals.
Pupa (plural, pupae)	A stage of complete metamorphosis in which the insect's body changes dramatically from the larval form to the adult form.
Resources	Things an animal needs to survive—food, water, shelter, etc.
Sample	A small number of observations used to infer information about a larger population.
Social insects	Insects that live in groups and care for their young.
Spinnerets	Silk-producing organ on the tip of a spider's abdomen.
Spiracle	A hole in an insect's body that allows air into the respiratory system.
Taxonomy	The naming and classification of organisms.
Thorax	Middle body region of an insect. Legs and wings are attached here.
Trachea	Branching tubes through an insect's body that carry oxygen to cells.
Trial	A test that is repeated in an experiment.
Warning colouration	Bright colours that warn predators an animal is poisonous.

About the Author

I have been teaching about insects and other aspects of the natural world for over 25 years. I have a Master's degree in Entomology, and my thesis research focused on teaching integrated pest management in the high school greenhouse.

I spent several years at The Pennsylvania State University, where I co-taught the educational methods courses Teaching With Insects and Bug Camp for Teachers. I also co-taught Bug Camp for Kids and Advanced Bug Camp for Kids, and helped organise a range of outreach programmes, including The Great Insect Fair.

Upon moving to New Zealand, I started The Bugmobile, delivering science outreach programmes with live insects to schools and preschools throughout Canterbury.

Today, I write full-time, spinning tales for children and young adults, and blogging about rural life.

Please visit me on-line at:
    Twitter: @RobinneWeiss
    Facebook: www.facebook.com/CrazyCornerFarm/
    WordPress: robinneweiss.wordpress.com

www.ingramcontent.com/pod-product-compliance
Lightning Source LLC
Chambersburg PA
CBHW042218240426
43670CB00035B/42